WALKING

WALKING

One Step at a Time

Erling Kagge

Translated from the Norwegian by
BECKY L. CROOK

Pantheon Books · New York

Grateful acknowledgment is made to the following for permission to reprint previously published material: Lyrics from "Walking and Falling" by Laurie Anderson, copyright © 1982 by Laurie Anderson and Nonesuch Records. Reprinted by permission of Laurie Anderson.

Excerpt from "To the Foot from Its Child" by Pablo Neruda, translated by Jodey Bateman, originally published in Argentina as *"Al pie desde su niño"* in *Estravagario* by Editorial Losada, Buenos Aires, in 1958. Copyright © 1958 by Pablo Neruda.

Library of Congress Cataloging-in-Publication Data
Name: Kagge, Erling, author.
Title: Walking : one step at a time / Erling Kagge ; translated by Becky L. Crook.
Other titles: Å gå. English
Description: New York : Pantheon Books, 2019. "Originally published in Norway as Å gå: Ett skritt av gangen by Kagge Forlag AS, Oslo, in 2018."
Identifiers: LCCN 2018035901. ISBN 9781524747848 (hardcover). ISBN 9781524747855 (ebook)
Subjects: LCSH: Kagge, Erling. Walking. Explorers—Norway—Biography. Meditations.
Classification: LCC GV199.5 .K34 2019 | DDC 796.51—dc23 | LC record available at lccn .loc.gov/2018035901

www.pantheonbooks.com

Jacket design by Jenny Carrow

Printed in the United States of America
First American Edition
9 8 7 6 5 4 3 2 1

For my mother and father who took me walking,
and for Ingrid, Solveig and Nor

You're walking. And you don't always realize it
But you're always falling
With each step, you fall forward slightly
And then catch yourself from falling . . .

—Laurie Anderson, "Walking and Falling"

I

One day, my grandmother was no longer able to walk.

That was the day she died. Physically, she continued to live a little longer, but her new knees, which had surgically replaced the old ones, were worn out and no longer able to carry her body. The remaining strength in her muscles wasted away from the days spent lying in bed. Her digestive system began to fail. Her heartbeat slowed down and her pulse became uneven. Her lungs took in less and less oxygen. Towards the end, she was left gasping for air.

In those days I had two daughters at home. The youngest, Solveig, was thirteen months old. As her great-grandmother slowly shrank into a fetal position, Solveig felt it was high time she learned how to walk. Arms raised above her head and hands clasped around my fingers, she managed to totter across the living-room floor. Each time she let go and attempted a few steps on her own, she would discover the difference between what's up and what's down, what's high and what's low. When she stumbled and smacked her forehead on the edge of the living-room table, she learned that some things are hard and others soft.

Learning to walk may be the most perilous undertaking of our lives.

Arms outstretched to keep her balance, Solveig soon mastered the feat of walking across the living-room floor. Spurred by her fear of falling, she took short, staccato-like steps. Observing her first attempts, I was surprised at the way she spread her toes, as though trying to grab on to the floor. "A child's foot doesn't know it's a foot yet," it wants to be a butterfly or an apple, writes the Chilean poet Pablo Neruda at the start of his poem "To the Foot from Its Child."

All of a sudden, Solveig was moving with more confident steps. Through the open terrace door and out into the garden. Her naked feet now came into contact with something more than flooring: the Earth's surface—grass, stone and, soon, tarmac.

It was as though a small part of her personality— her temperament, curiosity and will—became more apparent when she walked. When I observe a child learning to walk, it feels as if the joy of exploration and mastery is the most powerful thing in the world.

Placing one foot in front of the other, investigating and overcoming are intrinsic to our nature. Journeys of discovery are not something you start doing, but something you gradually stop doing.

When my grandmother—I called her my *mormor*—was born in Lillehammer, ninety-three years before Solveig, her family still relied on their feet as the primary mode of transport from one location to another. Mormor could take the train if she wanted to travel very long distances, but she didn't have many reasons to leave Lillehammer. Instead, the world came to her. Throughout her youth she bore witness to the arrival of mass-produced cars, bicycles and aeroplanes in her region of Oppland. Mormor told me that my great-grandfather asked her to accompany him down to Mjøsa, the biggest lake in Norway, to watch an aeroplane together. She told the story with such rapture that it felt as if it had taken place the day before. The skies were—suddenly—no longer solely the realm of birds and angels.

*

Homo sapiens have always walked. Since the time they first made their way from East Africa over 70,000 years ago, our species' history has been defined by *bipedalism*. Walking on two legs laid the foundation for everything we have become today. Our kind crossed over Arabia, continued on foot up towards the Himalayas, spread eastward throughout Asia, across the frozen Bering Strait through the Americas, or south towards Australia. Others walked west to Europe and, finally, all the way up to Norway. These first peoples were able to travel long distances on foot, to hunt in new ways over larger areas, and to gain new experiences, and learned from them. Their brains developed more rapidly than those of any other living creatures. First we learned to walk, then we learned to make fire and to prepare food, and then we developed language.

Human languages reflect the idea that life is one single, long walk. In Sanskrit, one of the world's oldest languages, originating from India, the past tense is designated as the word *gata*, "that which we have walked," and the future is *anāgata*, "that which we have not yet walked. This word *gata* is related linguistically to the Norwegian word *gått*, meaning "walked." In Sanskrit, the present is indicated by something as natural as "that which is directly in front of us," *pratyutpanna*.

*

I have no idea how many walks I've been on.

I've been on short walks; I've been on long walks. I've walked *from* villages and *to* cities. I've walked through the day and through the night, from lovers and to friends. I have walked in deep forests and over big mountains, across snow-covered plains and through urban jungles. I have walked bored and euphoric and I have tried to walk away from problems. I have walked in pain and in happiness. But no matter where and why, I have walked and walked. I have walked to the ends of the world—literally.

All my walks have been different, but looking back I see one common denominator: inner silence. Walking and silence belong together. Silence is as abstract as walking is concrete.

Before I got a family, I never wondered why walking was important. But the kids wanted answers: Why do we have to walk, when it's faster to drive? Even adults had questions: What is the point of moving *slowly* from one place to another?

*

Until now, I have tried the obvious explanation, the one you turn to because it's quick and easy and the opposite of the essence of walking, which is slowness: I explain that he who walks lives longer. The memory sharpens. The blood pressure falls. Your immune system gets stronger. But each time I said it, I knew it was only half the truth. To walk is something much larger than a list of advantages you can read in an ad for vitamins. So what is the other half of this truth?

Why do we walk? Where do we walk from and what is our destination? We all have our own answers. Even if you and I walk next to each other, we can experience the walk differently. After having put my shoes on and let my thoughts wander, I am sure of one thing— to put one foot in front of the other is one of the most important things we do.

Let us walk.

*

II

Everything moves more slowly when I walk, the world seems softer and for a short while I am not doing household chores, having meetings or reading manuscripts. A free man possesses time. The opinions, expectations and moods of family, colleagues and friends all become unimportant for a few minutes or a few hours. Walking, I become the centre of my own life, while completely forgetting myself shortly afterwards.

It is a truth universally acknowledged that one saves time travelling only two hours from one point to another instead of spending eight hours on the same journey. While this holds up mathematically, my experience is the opposite: time passes more quickly when I increase the speed of travel. My speed and time accelerate in parallel. It is as if the duration of a single hour becomes less than a clock-hour. When I am in a rush, I hardly pay attention to anything at all.

When you are in a car *driving* towards a mountain, with small pools, slopes, rocks, moss and trees zooming past on all sides, life is curtailed; it gets shorter. You don't notice the wind, the smells, the weather, nor the shifting light. Your feet don't get sore. Everything becomes one big blur.

And it isn't only time that grows smaller as one's pace increases. Your sense of space does too. Suddenly you find yourself at the foot of the mountain. Even your sense of distance has been stunted. Having travelled far, you may be tempted to feel like you've experienced quite a bit. I doubt that's true.

If you were to *walk* along the same route, however— spending an entire day instead of a half-hour, breathing more easily, listening, feeling the ground beneath your feet, exerting yourself—the day becomes something else entirely. Little by little, the mountain looms up before you and your surroundings seem to grow larger. Becoming acquainted with these surroundings takes time. It's like building a friendship. The mountain up ahead, which slowly changes as you draw closer, feels like an intimate friend by the time you've arrived. Your eyes, ears, nose, shoulders, stomach and legs speak to the mountain, and the mountain replies. Time stretches out, independent of minutes and hours.

And this is precisely the secret held by all those who go by foot: life is prolonged when you walk. Walking expands time rather than collapses it.

*

I almost always choose the simplest of two or more alternatives: whatever requires the least amount of time. Or is the most convenient. Or the warmest. Even when I know that the other possibility might be the better choice. Some days I choose the path of least resistance from the moment I get out of bed until the moment I get back in. Indeed, I can do it for days in a row. It bothers me.

Making things a little bit inconvenient gives my life an extra dimension. For as long as I can remember, there's been a little devil inside of me who constantly tells me to choose the path of least resistance: to take a shorter walk than planned, to skip out on visiting a sick friend and go to a café instead, to put off getting out of bed when I should. If, for example, you're accustomed to taking the car to get around, it can seem hard not to. It's simply too comfortable.

Constantly following this little voice seems like a way of escaping from the world and is a misuse of the opportunities that life presents to us. The philosopher Martin Heidegger pointed out that it's easy for us to end up having a slave-like relationship with this sort of devilish persuasion. Always giving in to it might mean that we become even further entrenched, both legs stuck fast in a deep, soggy swamp. Heidegger differentiates between what it means *to live* in this manner versus *to lead* one's life. Humans should, as the philosopher maintains, be willing to burden themselves in order to be free. If you always choose the path of least resistance, the alternative that offers the fewest challenges will always take priority. Your choices will be predetermined and you will not only live un-freely, but also lead a dull life.

So much in our lives is fast-paced. Walking is a slow undertaking. It is among the most radical things you can do.

*

It might be taking it too far to recommend that someone walks in the wrong direction or deliberately gets lost, but I think such advice could have its benefits.

In 1987, I trekked through the mountain range of Jotunheimen and climbed Store Skagastølstind, Norway's third-highest mountain, together with my girlfriend. She was a skilled climber and led the way up. However, just as we reached the summit, we were surprised by sleet and bad fog. Steep cliffs surrounded us on all sides. Going an extra step into the mist could be fatal and we were forced to spend the night up there on a small plateau. Without a tent or sleeping bag. Throughout the night, we jumped up and down to stay warm, shadow-boxed and flailed our arms. We still froze. Today, when I think back to that hike, I remember it as one of the happiest experiences that we shared together. Spending the night together under such dramatic conditions made this night stand out in my memory from all the other, easier evenings. When the sun rose and we helped each other descend to safety, we found that the hours spent in the darkness had brought us closer together.

I've lost my way so many times that I wonder whether I'm secretly drawn to the unknown and enjoying the little mystery of not knowing where I am. When I'm using Google Maps I always know my position and, at times, I end up looking more at the screen than at my surroundings. If I leave my phone at home and lift my gaze, I'm present. The world becomes larger. Suddenly, I get to know a neighbourhood, a city, a forest.

My brother, Gunnar, once said when we, as kids, had lost our way in the Østmarka forest: "I got lost here before, so now I know where we are."

*

It's common to believe that people locked up in prisons are the ones who move the least. But it's not that simple. Three-quarters of all English children spend less time outdoors than prison inmates of the same country; every fifth child is largely indoors all day; and every ninth child has not set foot in a park, forest or on a beach in the course of the entire year. Their time is spent indoors in front of a screen.

According to reports by the *Guardian* newspaper, many English parents say they know the value of playing outdoors but they don't feel able to influence their children. Staying indoors means not having the ability to enjoy the wonders of nature, such as seasons, animal life, sun, rain, trails and where we are.

Outdoor activity in the UK is also linked to social class. According to a 2016 study carried out by the Wildfowl and Wetlands Trust (WWT), the chances are a lot higher that a child spends less time outside if they are raised in conditions of poverty.

*

In cities with substantial poverty my experience is that the rich separate themselves from the poor by not having to walk in the streets. A thick, soupy smog envelops Delhi every winter. The well off can stay inside their cars as the air outside is filled with high concentrations of fumes, small particulate matter and ground-level ozone, while children walk to school in the morning covering their faces. A million deaths in 2015 were attributed to India's air pollution.

*

About seventy-five steps outside my front door, I walk past an oak tree. I can remember the changes this oak undergoes over the course of a year. In the dim, predawn light of winter, the leafless tree can appear like a monster. Later on, in daylight, it looks friendlier. At the tree's crown and in its bark and wood there are individual microclimates with hundreds of different insects, fungi, lichens and mosses all living their own lives. With spring come the leaves, the colours. The oak, the tree which according to legend takes 500 years to live and 500 years to die, straightens its spine and, with each toss of wind, disperses its pollen. I cannot see it, but I know that this is when the sap rises.

What I do see if I am driving in rush-hour traffic is the car up ahead moving too slowly, and a pedestrian walking straight out in front of me while sending a text on her phone. These are the types of things that irritate me. I sometimes even look over at the other drivers who are stuck in the same line of cars and think ill of them, since they—like me—are wasting their

time sitting in traffic. To this day, I have never seen a
single happy driver in rush-hour traffic.

Whenever I drive fast, through tunnels or on
highways, everything looks the same as it always does.
And by the time I've arrived at my destination, it feels
as though I've experienced nothing. High speed is a
menace to my memory, because memory depends on
time and spatial awareness, both of which are
truncated within the confines of a fast-moving
vehicle. Voices and music on the radio become just
noise. The hits all sound the same, as does the news—
confident voices claiming one thing in the morning
and something else before lunch.

In his prose piece *The Walk*, the Swiss author Robert
Walser described the desire to be transported from
one location to another without experiencing it as
madness: "I never shall understand, how it can be
called a pleasure to hurtle past all the images and
objects which our beautiful earth displays, as if one
had gone mad and had to accelerate for fear of despair."

In the summer, the leaves of the oak display countless nuances of dark green on their upper surfaces, while their undersides gleam with a paler, almost blueish green. Their blossoms are so tiny that I have to look for them. I only spot them when I get up close.

To me it feels like the oak tells us never to forget to see.

*

One of my first childhood memories is from the time my father and I walked around distributing flyers in our neighbourhood. He was active in local politics. We spent an entire evening stuffing the flyers into hundreds of letter boxes. Prior to that, I had often ridden the tram along this same route, but now that I had to go by foot, the distances suddenly felt much longer. I remember the tendons in my knees firing. The world felt so much larger when I had to walk each yard instead of simply taking in my surroundings from the tram window where I usually sat. I began to feel the way in which the body, surroundings and imagination were connected. I could still fantasize about walking far, but that night I started understanding something about distances and toil.

Since then, here in Oslo where I now live, I have taken walks through most of the city neighbourhoods. From Vestli and Mortensrud to Holmlia, Røa and Holmenkollåsen. I wanted to know more about how people live in my city. Using weekends and evenings for my walks, I have thus become acquainted with most of Oslo. When someone now talks about Furuset, it's no longer merely a stop on the subway line but a place of familiar villas, apartment buildings, mosques and churches, as well as an ugly memorial to Trygve Lie, the first Secretary-General of the UN. My next project is to draw circles around places in which I find myself, say with a radius of one to five miles, and then to follow the circumference on foot all the way around.

Walking sometimes means undertaking an inner voyage of discovery. You are shaped by buildings, faces, signs, weather and the atmosphere. Maybe we were made to walk, also in cities? Walking as a combination of movement, humility, balance, curiosity, smell, sound, light and—if you walk far enough—*longing*. A feeling which reaches for something, without finding it. The Portuguese and Brazilians have an untranslatable word for this longing: *saudade*. It is a word that encompasses love, pain and happiness. It can be the thought of something joyful that disturbs you, or something disturbing that brings you plenitude.

*

In the morning, when I am about to transport myself from my home to the city, I can sense a kind of chaos. My thoughts and ambitions must first transition from the bed to the kitchen, then to packing the kids' lunches and finally to a circle of colleagues who want to make and sell books. These are two different worlds, and as I walk, I feel I have the gift of an additional stretch of time to transition myself from the one reality to the other.

Walking, I can stop whenever I feel like it. Take a look around. And then continue on. It's a small-scale anarchy: the thoughts that stream through my mind or the anxieties that I sense in my body shift and clear up as I walk. Chaos is king when I first strike out on my walk, but as I arrive, things have become more orderly, even when I haven't given a thought to the chaos as I've walked along.

If I choose to go by subway or car, my transition from home to the city happens so quickly that I'm unable to fully detach from my home life. When this happens, it feels like I end up bringing my home life with me into the office. At the end of the day, my head has to be tuned in to home life again.

I don't expect some great thrill on the way to work each morning but I do expect something. And there is almost always something of interest to give my thoughts pause or to observe. The distance between my house and my work is two miles, which in some ways is too short, but certainly better than if it had been only 500 yards. There is an old philosophical paradox that says you will never find something valuable in the street because if anything of value were to be lying there, it would already have been picked up by someone else. But when I look around me, I find there are valuable things everywhere.

There is the thrill of watching people. Small impressions solidify when I walk in the city. It takes an uncomfortable eternity to walk past the Rumanian beggar sitting on the wet pavement at Valkyrie Plass with a Starbucks paper cup in front of him and pictures of his handicapped child in his lap. Faces I don't know rush past, some happily listening to music from their white iPhone headsets, others looking despondent and anxious, as if they're worried about a sniper hiding on one of the rooftops.

Even if I walk on the same pavements and pedestrian zones where I walked the day before at the same hour, everything has changed. Some people I observe across the years and can see how they have aged through the spring in their step. Each new day that I walk, the oak tree has changed slightly, the paintings on the sides of buildings have faded a tiny bit more, and the faces that met me only twenty-four hours earlier have grown older. The changes are too small to notice on a daily basis, it all takes place much too slowly, but because I walk, I know that it's happening.

When the North Pole slants towards the sun it is summertime and the days stay bright almost around the clock. It's easy to spot every colour in the rainbow then. In a sense, it almost feels like they are foisted upon you. In the late autumn, when our half of the Earth is in shadow, it's the time of darkness. But, in fact, there are even more variations of blue, violet, red, black and yellow when the sun hangs low in the sky;

you just have to make a bit more of an effort to spot them. The summer colours are served on a silver platter. But to see them in the winter, it is sometimes necessary to concentrate. You must peer into the weak light and, after a few minutes, all manner of hues will reveal themselves. These appear richer than in summer.

If I have enough energy left over, I use it to guess at the thoughts of the people I pass, and what kinds of tasks are awaiting them. I have only seconds to follow a tired gaze under a baseball cap or wonder why a woman is smiling serenely to herself. In the afternoons, I watch harried people who I suspect must be the parents of small children on their way to daycare before closing time. I know how that feels. Or maybe they are simply stressed out, without being expected at any particular place or time.

Clothing can sometimes tell you a lot. Men sporting expensive suits and nicely coiffed hair look to me like lawyers on their way to the office. Yoga instructors have their own dress code. Priests in collars walk with their own slightly ceremonial gait, though I have the impression that priests maintain their way of walking even without collars on. When my neighbour, who is a military officer, walks around in civilian clothes, he is still a military man and moves in the same way that he does in his uniform.

> *How oft, amid those overflowing streets,*
> *Have I gone forward with the crowd, and said*
> *Unto myself, "The face of every one*
> *That passes by me is a mystery!"*
>
> —William Wordsworth, *The Prelude*

*

I bought myself a pair of white trainers to wear when walking around the city. White leather with white soles. Two thousand generations after our forefathers left the dusty savannahs to wander north through mud and dirt, the carpeted floors of my office are vacuumed, the floors at home are washed, the pavements are swept, and the subways and trams are hosed down. In Oslo you can walk all day and still your shoes can remain white.

*

"There is a secret bond between slowness and memory, between speed and forgetting," writes Milan Kundera in the novel *Slowness*. When I read this sentence, I recognize myself in his text.

Kundera describes a man walking down a street, trying to remember something he has forgotten. In this moment, he automatically reduces his speed. Another man, who is trying to forget an unpleasant experience that he has just had, does the opposite and picks up the pace without a second thought, as though he wishes to escape from what he has just experienced.

Kundera reformulates these examples into existential mathematics and two equations: "The degree of slowness is directly proportional to the intensity of memory; the degree of speed is directly proportional to the intensity of forgetting."

Kundera is on the verge of something that goes beyond memory and forgetfulness. The pace we choose when we walk can be decisive for how we think. I have tried substituting "memory" with "intelligence" in Kundera's equation. Intelligence can be many

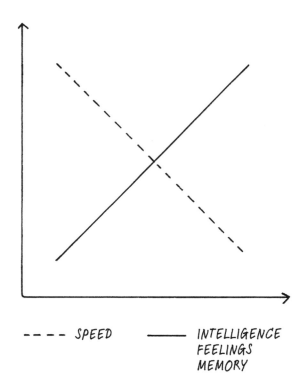

- - - - SPEED ———— INTELLIGENCE
FEELINGS
MEMORY

things but if you see it as the ability to think abstractly, as well as being able to apply earlier experiences to new situations, I believe that Kundera's maths works out well.

Emotions seem even less understandable than intelligence but it has nonetheless been a meaningful exercise for me to plug them into Kundera's equation. When I walk with a fast pace it feels like many emotions are held at a distance and when I slow down they return.

*

As one walks, unimportant thoughts and experiences mingle with deeply important ones. Something funny and something serious can be equally meaningful. A walk "refreshes and comforts and delights," claims the nameless author and main character in Robert Walser's *The Walk*, in response to the taxman: "Shut in at home, I would miserably decay and dry up." The taxman, meanwhile, thinks that the narrator should walk less and pay more taxes. The nameless character tries to convince him otherwise, claiming that his walks are critical for gathering material to write about. As a writer, I know that he is telling the truth when he says: "With the utmost love and attention the man who walks must study and observe every smallest living thing, be it a child, a dog, a fly, a butterfly, a sparrow, a worm, a flower, a man, a house, a tree, a hedge, a snail, a mouse, a cloud, a hill, a leaf, or no more than a poor discarded scrap of paper on which, perhaps, a dear good child at school has written his first clumsy letters." The taxman listens and thanks him for his reasoning. We never find out if the nameless author has managed to persuade him, but today it seems as though new generations have adapted to the accountant's ideal of sitting more, working harder and building careers.

Walser's character experiences "living poems" when he is walking. I myself am not as observant. Sometimes I talk on the phone or send text messages because I feel that my time is so valuable. In such cases, the walk is merely a mode of transportation. I am often fooling myself while doing this, overestimating my own value. Most of these tasks could easily wait for half an hour. Even 2,500 years ago, the slave Aesop, the fable teller, was already making fun of humankind's need to do several things at once—to multitask. According to the essayist Michel de Montaigne, Aesop—upon observing his master peeing as he walked along—is said to have asked: "What, do we have to shit as we run?"

*

When travelling, I only really feel at home in a new place once I've had the chance to see it on foot.
If I'm in a city I go up and down the streets. I'm letting my feet make maps. Just as I did when stuffing political flyers into letter boxes I could hardly reach. Trying to experience the place with my whole body rather than waiting until my eyes have taken in what my feet have already discovered. I discover new coordinates and get to know places in ways that are always changing. It is a personal form of topographical investigation.

Numerous cities feel like they were created for driving, but observing a city from a car window doesn't seem to be much different than looking at photos of the same city. In Los Angeles walking can get you stopped by the police, who are suspicious if you are on foot. "You walked?" This happened to me. Getting acquainted with places like this is very challenging, and that annoys me.

I decided to walk through all of LA with two friends. In order to get closer to the people and the tarmac. To get to know neighbourhoods with the soles of my feet.

From down below and up high. We planned to start at
Cesar Chavez Avenue at North Townsend Avenue,
walk 40 miles westward through Downtown, past
Union Station and then follow Sunset Boulevard past
Echo Park, Silverlake, Hollywood, Beverly Hills and
Pacific Palisades until the street ends in Malibu at the
Pacific Ocean. A walk you can do in one day but we
wanted to use four.

I had driven past the Scientology church located east
on Sunset several times before. A seven-storey, blue
V-shaped building that leaves a distinct impression of
just how rich and powerful the Scientologists are. The
building has become a landmark for tourists and
people living in the city. Each time I've driven past,
I've been awestruck at the thought of how many
members the church must have in order to fill such a
large space. On our walk through LA, we decided to
stop at the church, went inside, and asked for
guidance on how to live a better life. The interior
of the gargantuan building was empty, haunted-
house-like, with the exception of four representatives
from the Church of Scientology who seemed happy

to see us. The facade of the church was clearly not representative of its insides.

After a ninety-minute introduction on the history of Scientology, personality tests, as well as a private conversation with a representative from the Church, I was diagnosed with extensive personal problems, as were my two friends. The Church offered to help us.

Continuing westward towards the Pacific, we were struck by how few trees and how many nail bars and stoned people there are in Los Angeles. Everything is man-made over large swathes of the city. It is teeming with housing projects; we got the impression that half of the city's population polished the nails of the other half. The great pleasure of walking in a city is to be among the people. For the entire duration of the walk, you are what social anthropologists call a participant and not merely an observer. The divisions between what you see and what you do get smaller.

The physical distance from the Church of Scientology to West Hollywood—a part of Sunset that is dominated by old movie and new yoga studios, Fatburger and weight-loss centres, pill pushers and

prostitutes—is only a few miles, but the difference is substantial. West Hollywood, with its expensive cars, luxury hotels, restaurants and neon lights, appeared as a buffer zone between the haves, westward in Beverly Hills, and the have-nots.

Every day, 44,000 vehicles speed through Beverly Hills. In front of every house there is a sign that warns about armed response. There's no pavement in the part of Sunset that is called Dead Man's Curve. We had to balance between Mercedes and Porsches and the signs warning against trespassing. The too-close-for-comfort cars created a strong drag. It felt as though the thirty-five-miles-an-hour speed limit on Sunset must be the most violated in the Western Hemisphere. A few miles farther west we passed a makeshift memorial for thirteen-year-old Julia Siegler. She was run over by two cars when she tried to cross Sunset, on her way to school. According to *Variety*, the local magazine, "she loved dancing and the color purple."

After three days, I decided to experience my first pedicure in Rosie Nails in Pacific Palisades. As we sat there, having our stinking socks and trainers removed, two neighbourhood women drove up in their shiny, hulking SUVs and came inside wearing sleek yoga clothes. It was obviously their daily salon visit. Their pupils were dilated and their voices blunt. They may have taken oxycodone pills for breakfast and struggled to enter the salon without stumbling.

We had seen a lot of stoned people during our Sunset walk, but the two at Rosie Nails were the saddest of the lot. As my friend said: "Most of the others are not going to go on to pick their kids up from school."

I have been told that privileged Angelenos drive Hummers and SUVs so they can sit high enough above the street to avoid seeing the homeless people down below, but this isn't quite how I experienced it from the sidewalk. My impression, after briefly getting to know LA junkies, actors, artists, bartenders and police officers, is that everyone in the City of Angels wants only to meet someone more successful than themselves, so they don't have the capacity to notice others who are down on their luck.

When I meet so many different people within such a short time span, and with all the variety that LA has to offer, I think about how similar we all are, in spite of everything. Each of us possesses elements of beauty, idiocy, intelligence, goodness, evil, weakness, strength, optimism and pessimism; we all go through the trials of winning and losing.

As we walked, we tried to find a natural rhythm for walking and observing—without much success. There's no perfect speed for walking through a city; your pace varies according to the complexity of the area, the traffic, the absence or presence of sidewalks, the number of people who cross your path, and how many memories you wish to take home afterwards. Your brain's cortex sifts out what's important from what's unimportant, and then needs time to see and interpret those impressions. It's like reading a book. What we perceive depends on our attention, which is, after all, a limited resource. If you increase your pace, you automatically begin to concentrate on fewer impressions. In such instances, as the neurologist

Kaja Nordengen told me, you can "see without seeing and hear without hearing."

If I were to include all of the times that we stopped as we walked through LA, our average walking pace would linger somewhere around 1.2 miles per hour.

*

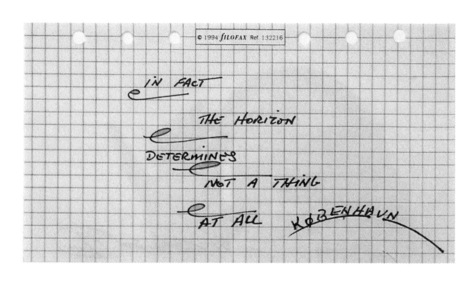

IN FACT

THE HORIZON

DETERMINES

NOT A THING

AT ALL   KØBENHAVN

In the 1970s, I learned early on that God banished Adam from the Garden of Eden. That image from a schoolbook, of a naked Adam abandoning Paradise with his head hung low, is one of the few things I remember well from my first six years of school. Since that time, however, I've come to believe another version of the story. Namely, that Adam wasn't chased out of Paradise.

There was nothing for Adam and Eve to do. Eve was curious and wanted to discover what would happen if her man ate from the tree of knowledge, and she lured him into it. The snake in Paradise was right when he told them about the dangers of eating from the magic tree; they would learn the difference between good and evil.

Immediately following their decision, they "heard the sound of the Lord God walking in the garden in thc cool of the day," and they both hid. These words are one of the world's earliest literary descriptions of walking. The first time I heard this sentence—I might have been seven years old—

I pictured God walking through the lush garden searching for the couple. A resigned old man in a worn-out tunic, with a big beard and long, shaggy hair, walking at an easy pace. I like that thought. God wandering through the Garden of Eden. Even God enjoys taking an evening stroll.

This story reminds me of the challenges of my own daily life. The perfect society can look great in ads for toothpaste and cars, but I find it unbearable in reality. Everyday life often lacks a single crucial feeling: *excitement*. Feelings like hope, love and joy become too similar—like we're collectively on Valium. I guess that Adam and Eve shared this same frustration—lack of excitement in their everyday life. The Bible does not say much about what happened to Adam after he became the first explorer of all time. We can assume that he didn't live "happily ever after." In Paradise, he was probably bored out of his mind. Outside of Paradise, he escaped boredom, but acquired a lot of new problems. However, Adam must have experienced a great deal of pleasure after he had walked for a while and then realized that he could just keep right on walking for as long as he wished. The gnawing restlessness that had plagued him in Eden gradually dissipated. A new sense of excitement must have taken its place.

*

I have walked on the same Dublin and Oslo streets as the characters in James Joyce's *Ulysses* and Knut Hamsun's *Hunger*. A story like *Hunger* is viewed differently after you yourself have walked through the same surroundings as the nameless, hungry narrator, even if you have just eaten. "The entire street is a swamp, with hot vapours rising from it," was Hamsun's description of Karl Johan, Oslo's main street. The description still fits. Five minutes' walk away: "Outside a basement café in Storgaten I stopped, debating coldly and soberly whether I should risk a small lunch immediately." Storgaten today resembles Storgaten in 1890, the year Hamsun's book was first published. Homeless people are still walking hungrily along the pavement. Observations such as these are small signposts that can help me enter a larger reality—or fiction.

The author Vladimir Nabokov taught Joyce's novel *Ulysses* at Cornell University from 1948 until 1959. Over the course of its 736 pages, the main characters, Stephen Dedalus and Leopold Bloom, set out walking on one "ordinary" day, 16 June 1904, through the streets of Dublin, in and out of houses and up and down sets of stairs. Events that appear to be more crucial than their walk—such as the death of Bloom's son, Rudy, as an infant, and the fact that his wife has refused to have sex with him ever since the tragedy, as well as his father's suicide—are nothing but subtle undertones throughout their day.

In order to understand the novel and to be able to appreciate Joyce's authorship, Nabokov maintained that it wasn't enough simply to know that the characters were walking the streets of Dublin and what they were thinking about and doing. He required his students to imagine the way in which the characters walked, and the time of day during which they walked: "Instead of perpetuating the pretentious nonsense of Homeric, chromatic, and visceral chapter headings, instructors should prepare maps of Dublin with Bloom's and Stephen's intertwining itineraries clearly traced."

I like this advice. Bloom names every street obsessively, as if extending an invitation to the reader to escape the narrative and walk the city. Nabokov followed his own advice and made a map of the pair's itineraries with arrows, numbers and names.

I have studied his map, and have since walked the streets where the story plays out. He is right. Davy Byrne's, a pub that is mentioned in the novel, becomes something else once you have walked the same streets as Bloom to the pub and taken a swig of Joyce's preferred glass of burgundy for lunch. In this way, the experience of the novel changes.

Alexander Selkirk, the Scottish inspiration for Daniel Defoe's *Robinson Crusoe*, was stranded from September 1704 to 2 February 1709 on one of the Juan Fernández islands off the coast of Chile. The book about the lone Crusoe has captivated me ever since my parents first read it aloud to me. My father told me that the novel was based on a true story.

The particular island that Selkirk lived on has naturally been given a new name in later years: Robinson Crusoe Island. (Who can really blame the tourist office for looking out for their own economic interests?) In 1986 I sailed to this island from Bermuda via the Panama Canal.

I was surprised by how much of the island's terrain matched the descriptions in the book. I combed it for the locations that had been described by Defoe. Crusoe's lookout and the cave down by the ocean are both there. One day, I attempted a free climb up to the highest summit on the island. I wasn't successful, too many loose rocks, but managed to get high enough to see out over the island from a bird's-eye perspective. It dawned on me that the novel I had fantasized about actually included two stories. The first was the story that I had listened to as a boy back home. The second story was experienced as I felt with my feet how the reddish volcanic substrate changed from rocks, cliffs and grass at the seaside into thick vegetation, brambles and trees higher up, until one reaches the treeline about 3,200 feet above sea level.

I walked from the ocean's edge up to the lookout to gaze out across the Pacific Ocean the way that Selkirk and Crusoe did as they scanned for a ship on the horizon. The way up follows the terrain of a natural path, so I was most likely walking in Selkirk's footsteps. He hiked up the 2,000 feet of elevation in the hope that just that particular day he'd see the ship. It took four years and four months until the ship came. Perhaps, as the years went by, the hikes became one continuous disappointment? I don't know, but I want to think that walking, believing, disappointments and the view kept him alive. As long as he walked up that hill, there was hope.

Standing at the top, it wasn't hard to understand why he chose this particular spot. From this vantage point, it's possible to see for many nautical miles in every direction, but the lookout also offers another dimension. Gazing across the island and the endless ocean beyond, I could feel that the view must have supplied Selkirk with an inner strength, a spiritual power, standing there alone.

From the lookout, I searched for the beach where Crusoe discovers footprints in the sand—the turning point in his existence—but I could not find it. Before I left, I walked across the island in one last attempt but never came across that sandy beach on Robinson

Crusoc Island. Neither did Selkirk find the comfort of sand under his feet, so he turned into a barefooted devil. The soles of his feet got so hard that when he was finally rescued, the sailors were shocked to see him chasing a goat on the rocky shore, overtaking it in a tackle and ending its life.

*

Your feet are your best friends. They tell you who you are.

The feet are in dialogue with your eyes, nose, arms, torso, and with your emotions. This dialogue often takes place so fast that the mind is unable to keep up. Our feet help us to proceed with precision. They can read the terrain, and also what hits them from underneath the soles; they process each impression, in order to take one step forward or one to the side.

Feet are strong and complex mechanical structures. With 26 bones, 33 joints, and more than 100 tendons, muscles and ligaments, the feet hold our bodies upright and in balance. Their development started long before our prehistoric ancestors even began walking upright. The changes occurred so that we could adapt to survive, but over time—over two million years ago—everything that Norwegians once did for survival gradually became something that we did more for pleasure. These things—walking across a field, up a mountain and along a cliff, or into the forest to find a spot for making a campfire—are most pleasurable precisely when we no longer *need* to do them. The feet that were developed to help humankind survive, and still are vital for survival in a major part of the world, have become tools for finding the perfect spot on the beach, or for taking a detour home, or tiptoeing into the bedroom, or walking away from our problems.

Nevertheless, the head can sometimes lose contact with the feet. An acquaintance of mine, who used to work long, demanding days as a lawyer, enjoyed her work until she hit the wall, had a panic attack, and thought she was going to die. After a long period of medical leave, she returned to her full-time job, only to experience another panic attack and an intense headache shortly afterwards. Her doctor referred her for psychomotor physiotherapy. During her first session, she was asked to stand up straight. The therapist asked her what she felt. Nothing. The therapist asked what she felt beneath her feet, in her legs, and in her thighs. It was only upon clenching the muscles in her thighs that she was able to feel she was more than merely an aching head. My friend the lawyer was then instructed to sit on a chair with her feet on top of two wooden pins, allowing them to roll beneath her soles. The therapist again asked what she felt.

"Feel?" The lawyer was irritated at the repeated question, since her answer always remained the same. Nothing.

The following week, she began to feel an enormous pain beneath her feet. She was instructed to stand up on the pins and to roll her feet back and forth. The pain became so intense that she collapsed into a spasm.

The lawyer later understood that the therapist had given her these exercises in order to allow her head to get back in touch with her body. Her head needed to come back down to earth.

*

The way you walk can also reflect how you *feel*. Minuscule deviations from your customary gait can tell the surrounding world whether you are having a good or a bad day.

Professor Rory Wilson of Swansea University has researched the degree to which illness, hormones, nutrition and emotions affect the movements of both humans and cockroaches. In the experiments, humans and cockroaches both had measuring instruments attached to their bodies, noting their patterns of movement across three dimensions. The purpose was to show coherent differences in the movements of the two species depending on their moods. To achieve the best results, all the experiments were conducted in the subjects' daily surroundings and not in laboratories.

According to the research, humans move about differently after watching a movie depending on whether the movie was sad or funny. This is apparent in other situations as well. When I see people before they head out on a walk through the forest, in the mountains or in a park, and then happen to see them again as they head home, I can tell that they have changed. This change is even more obvious to me than the change after going to the cinema. If people are exhausted after their working day when heading out for a hike, they are exhausted in a completely different way upon their return. Their eyes may be glowing, their step has a spring to it, and their smiles are more relaxed.

I have been in close proximity to cockroaches before, and so could scarcely believe that these creatures might have a well-developed body language, but I was wrong. Both healthy and sick cockroaches were manipulated by the researchers to run two yards per day. A healthy cockroach puts its feet down in a different way than a cockroach that is sick, and its posture is more resilient. A healthy cockroach also accelerates faster than a sick one. Polar bears consider the way another polar bear walks in order to decide whether it's a suitable mating partner—or whether it would be better to have for dinner.

Whenever I feel rested or happy, my body straightens

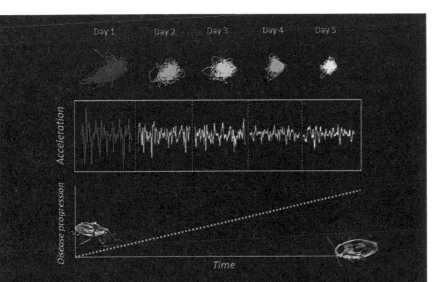

Even insects walk differently when ill – This is demonstrated by a cockroach infected with a fungus (and equipped with a smart tag to measure body acceleration 1,000 times per second). The animal shows less body movement (upper lines) as well as slowing and slurring footfalls (peaks and troughs in the middle boxes) as the disease progresses.

Your hips don't lie—*The way animals walk tells us much about their internal "state." The above two spheres visualize two periods of a penguin walking based on data acquired by accelerometers in a smart tag attached to its back. The more spread out the little cylinders are, and the warmer the colours, the more pronounced is the bird's waddling. The upper sphere shows the situation of a hungry bird, departing from its nest to forage at sea. The lower sphere shows the same bird returning to its nest, having eaten so much that it walks with a much more pronounced waddle.*

up and my steps become bouncier. It feels like I've discarded a heavy backpack. At times I feel happy without any particular reason, and this feels like an unexpected gift. The author Tomas Espedal touches on this in his book *Tramp: Or the Art of Living a Wild and Poetic Life*. The narrator is hung-over and depressed after drinking for four days straight, and then "the sunlight strikes a traffic sign and I am struck by an unexpected feeling of happiness." This small glimpse of luminosity causes his thoughts to become more and more lightweight, and "I slowly realize, you are happy because you are walking."

When I feel exhausted or downcast, I walk bending forward, with heavy steps. In his novel *Austerlitz*, W. G. Sebald describes the altered manner in which the citizens of Prague walked on the snowy morning when the German soldiers occupied the city: ". . . from that moment they walked more slowly, like somnambulists, as if they no longer knew where they were going." I don't mind that Sebald exaggerates. Even if the Czechoslovakians hardly walked like somnambulists during the occupation, Sebald is shaping an image that makes it easier for us to picture how the city suffered a kind of collective death that day.

My *mormor* always walked as though somewhat downcast. Her shoulders were hunched and her steps stiff, as though her muscles were unwilling to relax. Her life had been full of adversity. But I cannot remember her ever complaining. Quite the opposite. She was always loving and thoughtful when her grandchildren were around, though her body conveyed a much harder past.

*

A person's gait can tell more about them than their face. I only have time to glance at a face as I pass a person, but how a person is walking, putting one foot in front of the other, is something I can study for a while longer. If we happen to be walking in the same direction, I might even observe them for several minutes. A person's manner of walking is, of course, partly genetic—it didn't take long for Solveig's movements to remind me of her grandparents'—but it is also an expression of your values and social norms. The steps that Solveig takes for the rest of her life will convey something about who she is.

A policeman walks in a completely different manner than a hipster, who in turn walks differently than a beggar. Each of these three types of people, types who can often be seen on the streets of Oslo, is on a different kind of errand. One of these is keeping order, and his or her authority is reflected in the controlled movement of the body, another walks with a relaxed, ambling sort of gait, while the third has had to accept the daily indignities of their difficult life. Their social status has been internalized in their body.

"Everything in us is as if on command," claimed the French sociologist Marcel Mauss. It is simple to recognize a woman who has "attended convent school. She usually walks with her hands folded." Mauss gets very specific in his message, as French intellectuals often do, but he is right in saying that the way in which we move is a link between the psychological and the social system. One's social condition becomes, as his successor Pierre Bourdieu maintained, *inscribed* into our bodies.

Mauss and Bourdieu agreed that we will remain walking the way we do, but that this *may* change over time. Or suddenly, as when someone experiences a violent change in his or her life—sickness, unemployment or loss—but in general a priest, the police, a beggar, you and me will continue as we have always done.

*

The police in many different countries are trying to find out how to identify criminals based on the way bodies move when walking. By analysing movements, the hope is that we will in the future be able to conclude who the perpetrator is, with almost as much accuracy as analysing traces of DNA. Other studies have tried to analyse how offenders choose their various urban victims. The way that some people walk makes them look uncertain and vulnerable. The American serial killer Ted Bundy said that he could "tell a victim from the way that she walked down the street."

Your walk doesn't lie. However, you can bluff and teach yourself to walk in a somewhat different manner. If the potential victim switches to taking more confident steps, maybe a faster pace, and moves their arms, the perpetrator's interest *may* decrease. When I am walking through an area that I sense might be somewhat dangerous, I try walking with certainty in my step and a firmer rhythm in my torso. I don't really believe that anyone is scared off by seeing it, but I at least feel safer. On other occasions, when I pass someone on a dark street and notice that the person appears anxious—women seem to look instinctively over their shoulder when they go home alone in the evening—I slow my own speed and cross over to the other side of the street.

In the late 1970s, I saw the film *Grease* and in the days that followed, I tried to walk with the same swagger as Danny, John Travolta's character, when he goes soft on Sandy, the prettiest girl in the film, played by Olivia Newton-John. His was a broad, bouncing gait with arms following along rhythmically, but I didn't really succeed. A few days later, I returned to my own walk.

*

The theatre director Robert Wilson is deeply
fascinated by walking, and walking slowly in
particular. I asked him why.

As a director, Wilson is very concerned that all
of his actors walk naturally in every scene. If their
movements appear natural—most likely only after the
actors have tried and failed hundreds of times—the
director believes it opens them up to a new form of
creativity. An actor's creativity is not located in the
head, Wilson claims, but in the body. Once the
movements have finally become natural, he allows the
actors to practise their lines. Or to be silent. A raised
heel can appear more powerful than a shout.

"Time has no concept," he replied to my question.
"Very often, people say that in my theatrical work
people move slowly. If one should move more slowly
than one normally does and thinks of it as being slow,
it is one thing. But if one does not think about it, one
experiences *time* in a completely different way. The
body is full of many different energies that are
happening simultaneously, and every fraction of a
second will always be completely different. If one is

aware of this experience, it is a different way of thinking."

Wilson usually draws a detailed map on the stage floor outlining which actor should walk to which point on the stage, what pace they should have, and at what moment in time. The sketch is precise, practically down to the half-inch. Once all the actors have learned their movements and no longer require the map, he has it washed away.

Wilson understood early on just how complicated it can be to walk and what a person's walk can convey. When his little sister was born, his family learned that her feet didn't point straight out from the ankles but were severely pigeon-toed. This was at the end of the 1940s, in Texas. Her family chose to have her legs broken by a doctor, twisted to the correct angle, before being allowed to heal again. After one year in braces and a cast, his sister learned how to walk. "In watching her learn to walk, I had to rethink my way of walking. Our way of walking; a pedestrian walk. Her concentration was on balance, and how to put one foot down and moving the other foot forward, to control the movement without falling down. If one notices carefully the pedestrian walk, one will see that the step forward is always rather quick, which I believe is a fear from infancy that we will fall down if we do not get the foot forward quickly in order to balance. If one is balanced, standing on one foot, and takes time to put the other foot forward, the experience is very different."

There are 212 steps up to the publishing offices where I work. At least, I think so. I've counted them several times but I'm never quite sure, because I lose count every time.

In order to pull myself away from my daily grind— at times it seems as though I've been given a monkey-brain that always wants to do nothing other than hop around from one thing to the next—I decide to focus on each step as I go up. To lift one leg calmly and place it down in front of me. A little bit like Wilson's sister. I don't think about the next step but only focus on one step at a time, nothing else. It's difficult. When my thoughts start to race and I begin to think about the tasks waiting for me on my desk upstairs, I have a rule for myself that I have to go back down to the step where my thoughts were last focused on only the step and my foot. Or else I turn around and continue up the stairs, this time facing backwards. In the latter case, I suddenly feel helpless and, in this way, force myself to disconnect, to pause, shut out the past and the future. Even though my head just wants to focus on all the things on my work schedule.

At the top, seven flights up, I don't exactly understand what has happened. It seems as if I've been given answers to questions I didn't even know about.

Is it possible?

Socrates wondered about something similar: "But how will you look for something when you don't in the least know what it is?" Philosophers have pondered this dilemma—or *Menon's dilemma*, named after the sophist Menon, who asked Socrates this question—for 2,400 years. In 1942, the French philosopher Maurice Merleau-Ponty came up with what I think is a good answer to Menon, an answer that anyone who walks a lot could relate to: You think with your entire self.

He started with the assumption that the body is not merely a collection of atoms made of flesh and bone. We are able to perceive and care for our memories and reflections with our toes, feet, legs, arms, stomachs, chests and shoulders. Not only with our heads and souls, as Socrates emphasized. Merleau-Ponty understood something that neurologists and psychologists have since begun to study: everything around us is something with which the *whole* of you and I are able to have a running dialogue. "There is no inner man, man is in the world, and only in the world does he know himself." When we see, smell and listen, we are—in order to understand our experience—using the information that has already been stored inside our bodies.

If a bird sings while hidden in a treetop, I am unable to differentiate the sound that I hear and the bird that I picture to myself from other experiences that have taken up residence in my body. The birdsong that *you* hear is therefore not the same as that which *I* am

[75]

hearing, even if it's the same bird. Everyone has his or her own collection of experiences, and it may be that the information you have archived plays a larger role than the birdsong itself.

At the same time that Robert Wilson's sister was learning to walk, he himself was struggling to talk. He stammered so much that it was nearly impossible to understand him. As there was no speech therapist in Waco, where his family lived, his parents took him to see specialists in New Orleans, Chicago and Dallas. Nothing helped. When he was in his teens, he met a ballet dancer who advised him how he might learn to speak. Her advice reminded him of the way in which his sister had learned to walk. Once he began to say a word, the dancer told him, he shouldn't get stressed out or stop, but continue to try articulating the word calmly and at his own leisure until he had completed it. Yes, she said he could even spend several minutes saying the word "wwwwwheneeeeevvvver." The dancer had a basic understanding of how the body functions. "She said to me simply that I should take more time to speak, so I slowed down my speaking, and within a relatively short period of time, five or six weeks, I had overcome my stuttering. It was almost as if I had been speeding in one place."

In Wilson's performance piece *Walking*, it feels as though he has drawn on his childhood experience of things being allowed to take a long time. He and his audience take five hours to cross the Dutch island of Terschelling, a walk that usually takes only forty-five minutes. "I became more aware of my surroundings, and my perceptions were altered. Everything was different to what I would have experienced if I had been walking at a normal pace."

Sea air, birds, the wind, the sand, the stones, the horizon.

*

I tend to walk around in my socks or bare feet. Whether I'm at home, visiting someone or at the office, I take off my shoes. I do this in order to move my toes and to get rid of the thick layer of rubber that would otherwise be couched between my body and the ground. If I am sitting in a café, I prefer to keep my socks on and hide my shoes under the table so I don't have to deal with comments from an unhappy waiter.

I prefer to be barefooted, though it's not easy to do when you have a full-time job. I do this not only in consideration for my feet. To feel the wood floor, the cement, carpets, grass, sand, muck and tarmac. Or moss, pine needles and rocks. To feel the reflexes in each toe, the balls of my feet, heels and ankles improving. The skin on the bottom of my feet, with its nerves and reflex points—points that are connected to the rest of my body—are able to come into closer contact with the ground. Just as the body requires sunlight, the skin loves to feel the wind, and the ears delight in the sound of birdsong, the feet are liberated in this way. Naked feet are more vulnerable. I have to pay attention so that I don't step on anything sharp or trip on something hard.

The poet Pablo Neruda wrote, as I mentioned previously, about the foot that wanted to be a butterfly or an apple, but his romantic ideas end after a few lines. Later on in the poem he talks about how a child's foot must nonetheless relinquish its freedom and come to terms with a life spent in darkness, encompassed by plastic, rubber or leather, as it is tramped on the way into or out of stores and office buildings:

it hardly had time
to be naked in love or in sleep

*

For twelve years of his adult life the Norwegian philosopher Arne Næss lived directly under the Hallingskarvet mountain range at Tvergastein, a solitary cabin. Arne insisted on taking an alternative route each time the two of us would hike there, which sometimes meant shifting our path by mere inches from our earlier course. This was something all visitors had to do. Through all those years, Arne was determined that no one single path should lead up to his cabin.

He also decided that seven feet around the entire circumference of the cabin should be a nature reserve. In order to safeguard the heather, glacier buttercups and alpine dryad that grew there, visitors, including him, were only allowed to step on the rocks that lay within the protected zone. This allowed Arne every season to observe the living, undisturbed vegetation from his window.

Tvergastein may have been the only cabin in Norway without a man-made trail. There were a few animal trails a bit farther down the mountain, but nothing more. Today, eight years after he set out on his last journey, there is a single man-made trail that leads up to the cabin. Without Næss, hikers have unavoidably chosen the most convenient, and unchanging, route.

From his birth to his death, the Norwegian poet Olav H. Hauge lived on a farm in Ulvik in the fjord district of Hardanger. The farm is situated on the innermost part of the fjord, flanked by breathtaking mountains. Every hike that one might take among the steep terrain around Ulvik begins with a long uphill trek. Hauge's bookshelves were filled with literature from around the world, and the poet often walked around alone, in his mind talking about the books he had read and conversing with the authors who had written them. He describes this experience in the poem "Your Path."

This is your path.
Only you will
take it. And there's
no turning back.

There is *one single* path. It is your own, which you are creating as you walk, even when you walk on the same trails. But I think Hauge is wrong when he claims there's no turning back. You can always turn around, every minute of every day. The way back, however, will be a different one.

The Spanish national poet Antonio Machado sensed something similar when walking in the landscape of the windswept plains, oaks and hills around Castilla, "where the rocks seem to dream." He wrote nearly the same lines as Hauge in his poem "Wayfarer, there is no path":

As you walk, your way closes,
and when you look back
you see the path which your feet
never more will tread.

After reading Machado, Hauge noted the following in his diary: "FINALLY SOMEONE WHO AGREES WITH ME."

*

The British-Egyptian heart surgeon Magdi Habib Yacoub goes for a walk every day. One evening in the spring of 2009 we almost collided on our way out of a hotel at Lake Geneva. I can still remember the view laid out before us in the dusk light above the beautiful lake, mountains on all sides. We simply stood there, gazing. He told me that he was planning to walk two or three miles before going to bed, which had been my plan as well. So we decided to go together.

This was good fortune for me. I had not talked to Yacoub before, and I asked him about his profession. He told me that he had performed about 20,000 open-heart surgeries. Other doctors saw open the sternum for him and open the ribcage, and then the patient's heart and breathing are suspended for a brief period so that Yacoub can carry out the procedure within the heart itself before leaving the operation room and heading to the next patient, whose chest lies open and waiting. He usually has five operations per day.

Nine years earlier, he had given a two-year-old girl a

new heart. During the operation, he disconnected her own heart but left the organ inside her body. Eight years later, her replacement heart stopped working the way that it was supposed to. It was, once again, a matter of life and death, and Yacoub was summoned to operate. He disconnected the implanted heart and reconnected the girl's own heart, which had, in the meantime, grown and become healthy within her own body. It was the first successful operation of its kind. The girl healed quickly. Today she is married and has children.

I was curious and asked Yacoub what he had learned from studying thousands of beating human hearts. Yacoub replied, without much ado: "Go for a walk every day." He assured me that this advice would never grow outdated.

Yacoub said what my *mormor* must have felt. The father of modern medicine, Hippocrates, already had a grasp of this truth 2,400 years ago. He warned against being incorrectly medicated and emphasized that no medication could have such a broad effect as simply putting one foot in front of the other. "Walking is man's best medicine." I believe that walking has played a much more meaningful role in human health than all of the medicines that have been consumed throughout history.

*

When the Greek philosopher Diogenes was confronted by the idea that movement does not exist, he replied *Solvitur ambulando:* "It is solved by walking." Socrates walked around Athens conversing with people.

Charles Darwin went for a stroll twice a day and had his own "thinking path." Søren Kierkegaard was, like Socrates, a street philosopher. He wandered around Copenhagen—"I have walked myself into my best thoughts"—asked questions, wrapped his arm around people's shoulders and followed them for a turn, received an answer, released them, and continued on alone. Then he would return home, where he would rarely allow others to enter, and set down his impressions from the streets in writing.

Albert Einstein fled into the woods surrounding Princeton whenever he was frustrated with his work, and Steve Jobs went on walks with colleagues when he wanted to expand his ideas. Many of his successors in Silicon Valley conduct meetings as they walk, in the hopes of experiencing a similar effect. It works. We do that at my office too, although not often enough.

". . . the moment my legs begin to move, my thoughts

begin to flow," concluded Henry David Thoreau—it is too easy to give in to the worry that says other matters are more pressing.

I know there are people who are able to think clearly and run at the same time but I prefer a slower speed. When I walk my thoughts are set free. My blood circulates and, if I choose a faster pace, my body takes in more oxygen. My head clears. If my phone rings while I am sitting down, I like to stand up and pace about as I speak. My memory, concentration and mood improve after only a few steps. "If you are in a bad mood, go for a walk," was Hippocrates' advice. And if you are still in a bad mood: "Go for another walk." The context is reflected in our language. *Motion* and *emotion*. *Move* and *moved*.

Studies all over the world are conducted to find out how walking influences our creativity, mood and health. In other words: how our feet have an effect on our brains (and not the other way around).

At Stanford University in 2014, researchers found

that creativity increased by up to 60 per cent for those who walked for between six and fifteen minutes, compared with others who sat down for the same period of time. The two research leaders, Marily Oppezzo and Daniel Schwartz, got the idea for the study when they were out on a walk one day. "My doctoral adviser had the habit of going for walks with his students to brainstorm," Oppezzo said, about Schwartz. "One day we got kind of meta."

Sometimes when I am working, it feels as though my brain is on strike. I try to assemble my thoughts in order to make some progress, but find I am quite unable to do it. It feels like I'm banging my head against a brick wall. Instead of staying seated, I choose to go outside and amble about for fifteen minutes or so. At times, it doesn't seem to help much, but on other occasions it frees up my thoughts, and I can feel a bubbling between my ears, new solutions to questions that have been plaguing me.

The resurgence of new thoughts doesn't last, however. My feet assist me for as long as they are walking and for a short period afterwards, but then I have to go out walking again. No one is going to turn into another Steve Jobs just by walking, but the point, as expressed by the researchers in their rather cautious manner, is this: "Those that require a fresh perspective, or new ideas, would benefit from it, and '. . . it's possible that walking may allow the brain to break through some of its own hyper-rational filters.'"

*

The modern world is fashioned so that we sit as often as possible.

There are many arguments for sitting. Sitting is about the desire of those in power that we should participate in growing the GDP, as well as the corporate desire that we should consume as much as possible and rest whenever we aren't doing so. Our movements should be brief and effective. In the Stone Age, an adult human being went through 4,000 calories per day in order to cover the energy required to eat, to make tools and clothing, and to walk. Today, an average human being living in a rich country consumes, directly or indirectly, 228,000 calories a day, on goods such as food, clothing, communication and transport. The consumption of energy has become a full-time occupation, making it difficult to set aside time for walking more than just a few steps in a row.

It is easier for governments and societies to control us as long as we are sitting down. History is full of stories about those who did *not* remain seated and who thereby changed the course of history.

Walking can transform an entire country. When I read the history of France, it seemed that their revolutions began with demonstrators walking through the city streets. Gandhi and his followers proved that feet can be much more effective than a superpower's weapons. People joined together in walking and created a mass movement. The Salt March, a 240-mile walk led by Gandhi, forced England to give up its salt monopoly. The Rose Parade in Oslo, which followed the terrorist attack on 22 July 2011, was a gathering of 200,000 people. Marches by demonstrators are a red thread running throughout the history of advocating for better rights for workers, women and minorities.

What would happen if world leaders were forced to take daily walks among the people? For those who are in positions of great power, this can be complicated. A nice black car waits to pick them up. Those who are endowed with power separate themselves physically from the daily realities of everyone else, or in Kierkegaard's words: ". . . robbers and the elite agree on just one thing—living in hiding."

There is something undemocratic in distancing yourself from the natural world, the street and the people over whom you rule. In Norway, leading politicians fortunately walk among the electorate. They see us and we see them. They shop where we shop and have their coffee in the same coffee shops as those who put them in power.

Though you might be able to glean a lot of information from reading, listening at meetings, looking out of car windows, and peering down from your skyscraper, everything appears different if you walk along the streets where the citizens are gathering their own food for cooking, opening a shop, checking their phones, loving, reading, conversing and thinking. From far away, the world can seem homogeneous, but your mental map no longer matches the actual terrain.

The greater the physical distance between the decision makers and those affected by the decisions, the less relevant the decisions appear to the people impacted by them.

*

To believe that walking should never be painful is a misapprehension. I don't mean that you should be in anguish while pushing a buggy down the lane or going on a little evening constitutional, just every now and then. Nature has given us pain as an affliction but that's not all it is. Pain can also be beneficial and pleasurable, when it ensures that we recognize the feeling of well-being and, in particular, the *absence* of pain once it has receded. As the father of small children, you come to learn that great, everyday joys are reflected in toil. It is not a contradiction to be annoyed at having to change my children's nappies, or to be deprived of sleep night after night—I thought for a few years that each child would drive me mental— and to simultaneously love that same child. The pains and the joys are so deeply intertwined that they can be hard to differentiate. The philosopher Arthur Schopenhauer chose fewer words to express the same sentiment: "Only pain and want can be positively felt."

For Arne Næss, happiness had to do with *glow*—by which he meant fervour or passion—and *pain*. He distinguished between bodily and mental pain. Like a philosopher with a grasp of mathematics, he devised his own *equation for well-being*. The first time I saw the equation, I had to read through the logic several times because it is as ingenious as it is simple—and true:

$$W = \frac{G^2}{P_b + P_m}$$

W = well-being, G = glow (joy/fervour), P = pain, b = bodily, m = mental. Næss emphasized that G can be increased to whatever exponent you wish. This gives the equation a rather optimistic quality.

*

The equation assumes that a small increase in glow can outweigh a lot of pain. If you have very little glow for anything whatsoever, you will also experience little well-being, no matter how few inconveniences you might suffer. Næss told me that he wanted to point out the meaning of pain, while simultaneously spoon-feeding the belief that it is more valuable to increase one's *glow* than to reduce one's pain.

Næss's friend Peter Wessel Zapffe wrote—in his doctoral thesis with the classic name *On the Tragic*—on the importance of not taking short cuts, but instead using one's time to struggle towards a goal. Receiving too much technical help "is a reckless theft of humankind's reserves of experience." Big words, indeed. It's pointless to ride to the top of a mountain in a car or helicopter instead of hiking or climbing up, because the experience of standing on the summit is superficial if no pain was involved. Zapffe, himself also a philosopher, considered that our frequent need to simplify things acts as a censor on our opportunities to have great experiences. His basic idea, which I believe is shared by anyone walking long distances, is that *to achieve* is not necessarily akin to the value of *that which has been achieved.*

To take walks in fair weather alone—remaining indoors during wind, rain or snow—is to forgo half of the experience. Maybe even the better half.

   The father of the author Eleanor Catton, both from New Zealand, offered her good advice: "Nature looks more beautiful in the rain" and "A view needs to be deserved." He brought his daughter along on far more walks than she would have preferred, and she viewed his advice with ambivalence. I read about this father–daughter duo in a book written by the British author Melissa Harrison with the descriptive title *RAIN: Four Walks in English Weather.* Harrison's father, who also brought her along on walks, gave her somewhat different counsel of the same calibre: "Rise above it!" Overcome your exhaustion, the weather and the uphill slog. These three pieces of advice are not meant to be macho, but were lovingly bestowed in the hope that these men's daughters would have the chance to experience as many wonderful things in the wild as they themselves had. Our need for comfort not only implies that we avoid uncomfortable experiences but it also means that we lose out on many good ones.

*

For a period of six years, I only went on long treks.
To the North Pole, South Pole and the summit of
Everest. Even mountain climbers walk. First to the
foot of the mountain, then between the rock faces.
I was twenty-five years old when I began, and thirty-
one years old when I returned to walking shorter
distances. In all of these six years, I learned to delight
over the small things.

To walk is to enjoy simple pleasures. The longer the
duration of the trip, the more important it is to travel
lightly. Naturally. Even if I am only going on a Sunday
hike, I prefer to bring along only the bare essentials.
This might include a Thermos, some food and an extra
sweater. It took me years to realize that a single piece
of chocolate tastes better than an entire bar.

I always have a good feeling, a feeling of freedom,
when everything that I need in life is carried on my
back over the hours, days or months of the trip. It is at
times like these that I can eat and sleep wherever I
wish, whenever I wish. The next morning, there are no
8:00 a.m. meetings, and I don't have to go shopping

for dinner. The only thing that I start to miss over long periods of time is skin contact. To be hugged or to lie up close to someone.

It's possible to leave behind a whole slew of habits when you go for a long hike. There is pleasure in considering what you actually need. In having to decide between the things that you *must* bring along and those that you only *want* to bring because they might constitute a comfort. I have the impression that most people underestimate the amount of time that they would be able to make do with nothing more than a sleeping bag, an extra warm jacket, a small pan, a stove, matches and enough food. If you say it's impossible to survive with so little, and I say that it *is* possible, we are both probably right.

Some of the greatest pleasures that I have experienced in my fifty-four years of life are those that involve getting warm after I have been properly cold. In the forest of Østmarka and on long treks. "The distance between hell and heaven is short in these parts," Børge Ousland said on our way to the North Pole. The feeling of gnawing cold finally releasing its grip is the best feeling I know. I have drunk champagne in a comfortable living room in front of a fireplace but nothing tastes better than a glowing hot toddy when you're freezing out on the ice.

There is a thrill to not knowing what you may encounter as you walk. Your thoughts become more restricted. No one who wants to get hold of you knows where to find you. You are not living vicariously through other people. For one fleeting moment you can forget the rest of the world. Past and future have no role as you walk.

When Børge and I skied together for fifty-eight days to the North Pole, we didn't bring along any extra gear, only 44.19 ounces of tools. We repaired anything that fell apart along the way. The sole of my ski boot broke. My molar split. The only pair of woollen mittens that I had brought along wore out, but I laboriously repaired them every night before bed. Even though my fingers were cracked from the cold and the dry air, it felt good to pull the threads of wool in and out until the holes became tight again. Not only because I was happy to

have mittens for the next day, but because there is gratification in repairing the things you have.

We ate the same food every day. When you know that you are going to carry all of the food that you will eat over the next two months, you become very concerned about packing the most calories per gram of food: oats, fat, chocolate, raisins, dried meat and formula milk. Formula milk provides an extra amount of energy. It didn't taste very good at the beginning, but with each day that passed, and the more exhausted we became, our food began to taste better than the day before. Before we had even arrived at our destination, it tasted heavenly. Towards the end, we were so hungry that we diluted our food as much as possible with water in order to prolong the experience and to create the feeling of being full.

To ensure that Børge didn't get more than me, and vice versa, one of us would divide up the portions and the other got to select which one he wanted. "As hunger becomes a torment, dividing up and choosing your portion becomes a science," I wrote at the time.

*

Once, very close to the North Pole, I dropped a raisin in the snow during a short break. It's hard to get all of the raisins out of the bag and into your mouth when you're wearing huge gloves, so one of them slipped from the bag and fell to the ground. It was even harder to pluck it up out of the snow. I was so hungry and so ravenous for the raisin that I got down on all fours, lowered my head, stuck out my tongue and scooped it into my mouth. The feeling of joy from having the raisin between my lips, letting it roll around, and chewing slowly reminded me of something I already knew: it's important to be able to enjoy small bites. A little bit tastes good; even less tastes better.

Back at home, returned to civilization, daily life takes over with surprising speed. Pleasures become more complicated, often less intense and more to be expected. Over the course of a few days, grand sensations—such as feeling full or warm, sleeping well, or seeing another human being—are taken for granted. We have a saying in Norwegian: Much wants more. And that's exactly how it is. I try, with varying degrees of success, to continue enjoying small things.

To value the fact that I am at home in my living room, that I can participate in my own family life, and to be happy about those things that I missed while I was away. But the pleasure of savouring a single raisin seems absurd when I have an entire packet of raisins in a cupboard in my kitchen and the fridge is full of other good food. As I mentioned earlier, I know that a single piece of chocolate tastes better than an entire bar, but I still eat the entire bar.

*

To take a walk through nature, and find a quiet place to lie down when I am tired—this is one of the most delightful things one can experience. To look up at the trees that rise up around me, to simply relax. In Japan, they gave a name to this in 1982: *shinrin-yoku*, which means "forest bathing." A therapy—forest therapy—to help calm one's nerves.

Over the past few years, researchers at the University in Chiba have studied both the physical and psychological effects of trees. The results have, unsurprisingly, shown that forest bathing creates well-being and lowers stress and blood pressure. "We were made to fit a natural environment," concluded the researcher Yoshifumi Miyazaki, Director of the Center for Environment, Health and Field Sciences at Chiba University.

One finding that *was* surprising, however, was that researchers discovered that time spent with trees can strengthen the immune system, lower cholesterol levels, and act as preventative medicine. Particular types of trees and plants emit phytoncides, essential oils that are "exterminated by the plant" in order to protect it from bacteria and insects. Spending time around these plants causes us to take in the substance as well, and to benefit from some of the same effects, while gratifying all five of our five senses: the sound of birds, the smell of fresh air, the sight of green leaves, the physical closeness to trees, plants, moss and grass, and the taste of berries and mushrooms. A number of different therapy paths have been developed based on this and other studies in Japan.

Henry David Thoreau described *shinrin-yoku* in his book *Walking*, 151 years before the expression was penned: "I think I cannot preserve my health and spirits, unless I spend four hours a day at least—and it is commonly more than that—sauntering through the woods and over the hills and fields, absolutely free from all worldly engagements." He even claimed to be in love with an oak. Which is a good choice, if you have to choose a tree. "There was a match found for me at last. I fell in love with an oak shrub." Thoreau was so convinced by his thinking on the matter of trees and walking that he concluded by giving everyone who does *not* walk "some credit for not having all committed suicide long ago."

*

Michel de Montaigne tells a beautiful story about Kaiser Conrad III, who in 1140 besieged the town of his rival, Welf, Duke of Bavaria. Conrad did not want to show mercy and was looking forward to killing Welf and all his men. The only people who Conrad was persuaded to spare were the city's women. They were permitted to leave their homes, taking only as much as they were able to carry on their backs. The women were "gripped with rage, and decided to carry their husbands and children" on their backs. Even the duke was carried out in this way. Conrad was so impressed at seeing the women carrying the men and children on their backs that he "felt tears of joy, and his mortal hatred" faded.

I love stories like that. They remind me of everything that *could* happen, just over the horizon. I can imagine the women of Bavaria walking towards their enemies, battered by the siege, bent forward with short steps, bearing their beloved. It's the smallest acts—the miracles that happen every day—that fascinate me the most.

*

I walk away from my problems. Not all of them, but as many as possible. Don't we all? Some of my problems fade away as I walk. They might vanish within an hour, or a few days. Perhaps they weren't as big as I had imagined? It's often like that. Something that I view as problematic, that stirs me up, turns out not to be so troublesome or important, after all, once I have gained some distance from it.

Other problems disappear underfoot only to resurface once I return home. Problems tend to appear in a different light after a walk. I share the experience of the main character in Kathleen Rooney's novel *Lillian Boxfish Takes a Walk*. "Taking to the pavement always helps me find new routes around whatever problem I'm trying to solve: phrases on signs, overheard conversations, the interplay between the rhythm of my feet." Most of the people I know who struggle with big personal problems are those who don't take walks. Maybe I just know the wrong people, I can't be sure. Of course there are some problems that are so big that you can't just walk away from them, but most problems benefit from a healthy stretch of your

legs, a kick of endorphins and a release of stress,
allowing worries to go further away.

While we were preparing to go to the North Pole in
1990, we spent a few weeks testing our gear in Iqaluit,
a small town in the north-east, in the Canadian Arctic.
It was here that I learned about a valuable Inuit
tradition. If you are so angry that you can hardly
control your feelings, you are asked to leave your home
and to walk in a straight line through the landscape
outside until your anger has left you. You then mark
the point at which your anger is released with a stick
in the snow. In this way, the length, or the strength, of
one's rage is measured. The most sensible thing that
you can do if you are angry—a condition where our
reptilian brain rules our decisions—is to walk for a
while away from the object of your anger.

Twenty years after my visit to Iqaluit, I decided to
venture across New York, partly underground, with
the urban explorer Steve Duncan. We wanted to walk
through the city's sewer, train, water and subway

tunnels. From the Bronx, north of Manhattan, to Brooklyn and Queens and out to the Atlantic. My motivation was a spirit of adventure, but it was also a need to cleanse myself—to get *catharsis*—in muck and sewage. My home life felt like shit when I left. It was becoming increasingly clear to me that my partner, the mother of my children, and I were going to separate. My problems made me physically ill, my stomach full of pain.

I wanted to go on a pilgrimage. I wanted to suffer, to walk towards a target, and, for a couple of days, keep my familiar surroundings at a distance. My trip was not as risky as a pilgrimage of the Middle Ages could be, where robbery, hunger and being taken prisoner were among the expected outcomes. However, it was still a spiritual journey.

The walk was not along a common pilgrimage route either, such as one of my future dream routes to Santiago de Compostela, or around Mount Kailash. Friends of mine thought New York was a bad idea, but my thought was that literally diving into shit could be just what I needed. Maybe it would make my own problems appear less significant?

We began at 242nd Street and Broadway. After four days in and out of the city's mythological network of tunnels, Steve and I then came to SoHo and, in the middle of Greene Street at 3:30 a.m., we stood on either side of a manhole, and stuck our fingers into the cover to pry the shaft open. If they aren't pressed too firmly down by passing cars, manhole covers are surprisingly loose. We shimmied down and I pulled the cover back over our heads. It fell into place with a small thud.

Darkness engulfed us. I felt relieved that the police had not spotted us slipping below ground. We got out our torches and I switched on my air-quality monitor. The four main dangers in a sewer are poisonous and explosive gasses—particularly hydrogen sulfide (H_2S), or "swamp gas," as it is called, because the gas forms in stagnant pools—flooding and infections. Sewage can never be trusted.

The architectural wilderness of subterranean tunnels is a living organism; tunnels are built, extended, routes altered, new foundations constructed, new pipe systems connected to the old, and the underground terrain is constantly in flux. All of this takes place without the knowledge of those above ground, who never see what is happening.

Steve crouched and began to walk towards Canal Street, knees bent, back hunched, his arms in front of him to make his body as small as possible. The tunnel was only three feet high and three feet wide, made of cement. I followed. A stream of toilet paper, muck consisting of small chunks, unidentifiable objects and the occasional condom flowed downhill in the same direction, giving off a nice babbling noise. As I lowered the beam from my headlamp, it struck me that people in SoHo go through a lot more toilet paper than those up in the Bronx. Closer to Canal Street, the tunnel became lower and wider. Neither of us had expected the height of the sewer tunnel to decrease to only fifteen inches. I sank down towards the hard cement, placed my forearms and knees on the ground and crawled forward on all fours. The smell wrenched at my nose but it was no worse than changing my

children's nappies. The height of the tunnel soon slanted farther downwards and I was forced to lie completely flat and to wriggle in order to move. Above ground, the air was dry and fresh, but down here it was humid, and the warmth from the sewage wafted into our faces.

A colony of cockroaches covered the walls. They looked like the same cockroaches I have seen all over the world and I guessed that they were the basic *Blatta orientalis*. As I shimmied past, I thought of their rare talent for survival and their lack of talent for change. After 250 million years on Earth, they are apparently still the same primitive insect.

I inched along, my chest and back gliding into the ooze above and below me. My gloves, hat and jacket were plastered with slime. The distances that we were covering were small, but down in the sewers time follows another rhythm. Time ceases to matter. This is the same feeling that I have experienced on other expeditions and when I am together with someone who I love very much. In these moments, time seems either to speed up or go very slowly.

I stopped, lifted my head and peered down the tunnel. What was awaiting us farther ahead? For the first time in as long as I could remember, I asked myself: What am I doing here?

Of course, I should probably have asked this question much earlier—it's something one should often wonder—but the sewer is not a particularly good venue for pausing to philosophize, even if my current surroundings reflected my mental and emotional state before the start of my adventure. My problems, it turned out, had not disappeared when I returned home. On the contrary, they were too big for me to simply be able to walk away from. But I had taken a break from them.

Maybe the journey wasn't only about being somewhere else but also a desire to be *someone* else? When I was walking along in mucky clothes, disappearing underground, uncertain of what might occur at any moment, carrying everything that I needed on my back, I was not the same as I was back home. Normal was scoured away. I was not heading to meet anyone.

There was no mobile reception below the tarmac, and I didn't even know where I was going to be sleeping the next night. I began to believe that the world is not as it appears; the world is as you are.

Søren Kierkegaard claimed that every human being "stands at the crossroads." It's brutal to worry that every single thing we do is somehow transcendent. A new beginning. Even something seemingly trivial— such as balancing on the edge of a pavement on the way to the office as I walk, trying to guess at the thoughts of those who I pass, or pausing to give money to a beggar, or smiling at someone who looks sad— can change the world. With each step that I take, as the street philosopher wrote to his sister-in-law, Henriette Lund, in 1847, something happens.

"Above all, do not lose your desire to walk; every day I walk myself into a state of well-being and walk away from every illness," he wrote in the same letter, ". . . and I know of no thought so burdensome that one cannot walk away from it." This is sound advice, yet I know from my own life that it is hard to walk away from heartbreak. Kierkegaard himself experienced this as well. He never got over his broken relationship with Regine Olsen. In the decade after their break-up, which he himself had initiated, he tried finding the streets where he believed she walked in the hopes of meeting her, almost like a *stalker*.

His advice, unfortunately, had a limited effect on Henriette Lund. Kierkegaard apparently forgot that his sister-in-law was sometimes so sick that she couldn't even get out of bed, much less take a walk.

If a walk lasts for many hours or days, it takes on a different character than one that lasts for only half an hour. Your dependence on external stimuli decreases, you are torn away from the expectations of others, and your walk takes on a more internal character. After only ten days alone, heading towards the South Pole, I wrote in my journal on day eleven: "The feeling of being present in life is stronger here than at home. The loneliness is compensated by the thought of the goal and a feeling of being one with nature . . ." Though

Steve and I talked occasionally during our exploration of the New York underground, we most often walked in silence. There were so many noises in New York that I almost stopped noticing them. On the way to the South Pole, by contrast, the silence was so all-consuming that I could both hear and feel it. The silence there felt more powerful than all of the underground commotion combined, but the similarities between a polar trek and an urban exploration beneath SoHo are more important: both are about finding peace as you walk, leaving your problems at home, becoming a part of your surroundings, and being content to take one step at a time.

Is this culturally determined? I believe much of it is. If I had been born on one of the islands of Hawaii, I might have preferred surfing away from my problems instead of walking. If I had grown up in a family that practised Zen, I would have chosen *zazen*, sitting with crossed legs, quiet, deep in contemplation. In Buenos Aires, I may have danced the tango, another form of walking. I have surfed, danced and sat cross-legged at various times, but as I am Norwegian, walking is the most natural way. It helps too that this is one technique that I don't have to learn. It's something I've always done.

*

During the autumn of 1993, I walked through the Swiss Alps together with a friend. The sun was burning, we were exhausted, the sweat was dripping, and once we reached a small lake, my friend dived right in. I did the same, but while his dive was flat, mine was deeper. I hit my head hard against the bottom and was barely able to get back on to dry land. The first doctor to take a look at me was concerned I might have broken my neck and called the air ambulance to take me to hospital. In the course of the night, it became evident that my neck wasn't broken; however, I still had to stay in bed until I was able to walk again.

After a week, I noticed how my legs and arms had shrunk, and how my breath was more laboured than it used to be. I was surprised at how fast these changes occurred. I've since learned that this is just the way it is. In the research project *Dallas Bed Rest and Training Study* from 1966, five healthy twenty-year-olds were put to bed and told to stay there. When writing up the study three weeks later, the researchers claimed the young people's muscles and breathing capacity were at the levels of sixty-year-olds.

When lying in bed, I kept wondering what it would be like if I were never able to walk again. First the shock, then the sorrow, and then all the years to come. I was thinking that, with time, I would be able to adjust to such new circumstances. Maybe I would begin seeing the world differently, appreciating other things that I'd become used to? I soon realized that I didn't really understand anything about this at all.

The Norwegian author Jan Grue relies heavily on his wheelchair to cover large distances. Grue is also a professor and researcher on disability and the prestige ranking of illness. I went to see him to find answers to my question. We met in his Grünerløkka neighbourhood, where he lives, and rolled and walked up to Majorstuen, where he had an appointment with his dentist.

Grue said that it had been tough learning to use a wheelchair when he was seven or eight years old. "The learning curve was steep and I kept crashing into apple trees. But after a few months, I was able to master it, and after a few years I almost didn't think about the wheelchair as something external to me. It is, in many ways, an extension of my body." For Grue, self-determination and autonomy are the most important factors. To be able to move freely whenever he feels like it. Thanks to an electric wheelchair that he finally got the hang of, he was able to do this. It was only when we were crossing the roundabout at Bislett that we were both reminded of the limitations that he faces in the form of raised kerbs and bus drivers rushing to stay on schedule.

When we stopped to say our goodbyes at Majorstuen, Grue mentioned that his ten-month-old son, Alexander, was learning to walk. He talked about those first steps and the intense joy that his son must have felt at mastering the world, at *being in the world* in a new way: "Each body experiences pleasure in its own way, whether it is a child learning to take their first cautious steps, a wheelchair user who is able to move about freely, or someone walking. The essential thing is our experience of the world, regardless of the modality that takes."

*

Andrew Bastawrous was a teenager growing up in England when he came across an article about people who were blind because they had been without some quite simple medical assistance. Andrew decided then and there to become an eye doctor. Today, fifteen years later, he drives his mobile clinic from village to village throughout East Africa and offers his help.

One late afternoon when Andrew and his colleagues were closing up after a long day in a rural Kenyan village, a thirty-five-year-old blind woman named Maria arrived, carrying her six-month-old child. Andrew told me that it was "obvious that the mother was blind, not by her eyes but by the way she walked. There is a certain, searching walk that people have when they are in a new environment and are using every sense to navigate safely."

Maria had heard rumours that the doctor's van would only be in the village for this one single day. She lived several villages away and had started walking at dawn. She had never crossed a street with traffic by herself before. She told Andrew that it was "a terrifying experience." Not only could she hear the delivery trucks, cars and motorcycles zooming past her, but she could feel the air pressure from them as well. She stood for a while and waited for someone to help her cross, but no one came.

Maria decided to dash across the street during a quiet moment. A car came from the right when she had nearly crossed and she heard the blare of its horn, so she held tightly on to the baby, who was clutching her breast, and threw herself forward. Feeling the grass beneath her feet, she realized that she had successfully crossed the street and that both she and her child were safe for now. The next hours were "a blur, walking, tripping, crawling, asking for help" until she managed to locate the clinic. The child cried, and Maria was afraid.

One of Andrew's colleagues examined her eyes with a torch and saw that she had cataracts in both eyes. They operated the next morning. The procedure was quick, and by the end of the same day Maria was able to see well with both eyes.

She had never seen her child, and she lay gazing at

her daughter's smile, studying every movement and embracing her.

Maria was eager to get home to see her two other children and husband for the first time, but she didn't know how to get back. She had heard that there was a white sign in the ditch of the road near her *shamba*, the patch of earth where her family lived, but the place did not have an address.

Andrew's colleagues took her in the car to look for a white sign, without success. Maria was able to find her way when she walked, because she looked with her feet, but it seemed impossible when she was sitting in the car. They drove farther, but the road became a path and they were forced to get out of the car. Maria began to walk. Her feet once again recognized the way home.

Far up the path, several children were playing in a river. Maria stood watching them and asked: "Which are mine?"

Suddenly the children saw their mother. They sprang up and ran towards her. While she embraced them, she asked: "Where is my husband?" Everyone looked around, and suddenly they heard a man call: "Maria!" It was her husband. The sparkle in his eyes and the way that he walked emanated happiness. His wife could see him for the first time—a small miracle that had begun with just a few steps the day before.

*

It might seem pointless to lug 120 kilos of food, fuel and shelter with you for a couple of months when you could simply fly to your destination in a few hours. Or to wake up alone in –40°C when you could be at home in your own bed next to your partner. Or climb a mountaintop when there's a chairlift that will take you to the top.

"Because it's there" was the legendary reply of mountain climber George Mallory when he was asked why he kept attempting to conquer Everest. A good answer, that. The words tell us something about Mallory as a person, though not too much about why he wanted to reach the summit of the world's tallest mountain.

I like to believe that Mallory, in his own way, wanted to remind us that there are few things that we truly *have to* do in life. No one *has to* climb Everest, and there's hardly anything else we have to do either. There are many things that we *should* do or *could* do, but rarely something we actually *have* to. If you go for a long walk, you'll be fine; if you stay at home, you'll be fine as well. But when something is too easily obtained, it rapidly loses its pleasure. It has to cost you something in the form of icy temperatures, wind and steep slopes. The excitement is in the toil of moving in the right direction. Stretching out to reach a given point. Freezing. Regaining your warmth. Walking along the ridge leading to Hillary Step, where the mountain face plummets 9,840 feet down to Tibet on one side and 6,560 feet down to Nepal on the other. The uncertainty of whether or not you will reach your goal.

Mallory had another, longer reply, in which he nicely illustrates the insignificance of his greatest dream: "We shall not find a single foot of earth that can be planted with crops to raise food. It's no use. So, if you cannot understand that there is something in man which responds to the challenge of this mountain and goes out to meet it, that the struggle is the struggle of life itself upward and forever upward, then you won't see why we go. What we get from this adventure is just sheer joy. And joy is, after all, the end of life. We do not live to eat and make money. We eat and make money to be able to live. That is what life means and what life is for." One challenge is to consider that the kind of joy that Mallory mentions is short-lived. Following an expedition, none of the participants are eager to strike out again immediately. Their desire for another adventure might return after a few months or a year at home. Mallory always gave in to this desire.

The elated feeling one gets from reaching the summit of a mountain does not last very long either. Having arrived, when I was finally allowed to stop, drink some tea, and look out across the Himalayas, I felt moved and could feel a growing lump in my throat. I stood up tall and reached my arms into the sky. But my joy dissipated quickly when, after only a few minutes, I asked myself: "How the hell am I going to get down?"

George Mallory died as he lived, on Everest, in 1924. On the way up or down from the summit; there is no one who can say with certainty. He had brought a photograph of his wife, Ruth—who had once written in one of her letters to him: "I have more desire to grow old together with you than any other in the world. You have already made me into a better person"—to leave at the top of the mountain. When Mallory's body was later found, the photograph was not on it. He must have left it at the top, lost it, or forgotten to take it along. I always hope the photograph made it to the summit.

*

Paradise is where I am. This is the thought that arises when I sit at home in my living room with a good book, share a meal with people whose company I value, or go on a walk.

Such an agreeable state never lasts, of course. Even if our surroundings remain the same. Just as a disagreeable state won't last either. The reason for this is that even a continuation of a feeling will eventually cause a shift in your condition. Feelings of well-being are never infinite; they continuously have to be supplemented in order to continue.

I have heard sensible people compare risky expeditions to playing with death. I can understand why they think that such undertakings are meaningless. After all, it can seem absurd to willingly expose oneself to extreme cold, hunger and uncertainty—which in itself shows just how far we've come in terms of our affluence as a society—but to go on an expedition is not to play with death. It is the opposite. It is living a little bit more fully.

Before I start walking, I take as many measures as I

can to minimize risks. Then, when I watch the sun go down, step over a gaping crevasse, climb over a barbed-wire fence to enter a train tunnel, or stand face-to-face with a hungry polar bear, I am infused with a feeling of being present in my own life. Once again, paradise is where I am. Nothing else holds as much meaning as my life does in that place, in that moment. I wouldn't miss these experiences for the world. We seek out such dangers because the experience of intense situations, and our ability to overcome them, feels like a confirmation of our own vitality. A few dozen seconds stretch out like an eternity. Only the present moment matters when you are thirsty and happen upon a stream, or are hanging from a cliff, or sit perched on a rock studying the shifting clouds. The present moment and eternity are not necessarily opposites. Time ceases, and both can be experienced at once.

What I like most of all is to walk until I nearly collapse. To sense the pleasure, the exhaustion and the absurdity of walking all blending together, until I can

no longer tell what is what. My head changes. I don't
care what time it is, my head is devoid of all thought,
and I become a part of the grass, the stones, the moss,
the flowers and the horizon.

I wear myself out because I want to, not because I
have to. Break myself down physically. It's a nice
change from everyday life. To concentrate and
to be disrupted are not opposites. Both are always
present to various degrees, but if you have been broken
down, you no longer have the same strength to be
disrupted.

Before I manage to really wear myself down on a
walk, there is often so much to think about. Children,
work, unanswered messages. When my strength is
reduced, I no longer have the resources to think about
much, and that's when the smells, the sounds and the
ground seem to draw much closer to my experience.
It's as if my senses open to their surroundings. Nature
is transformed. A forest can become something new in
the course of a few hours. The moss is no longer
simply green, but now consists of endless shades of
green. Socrates claimed it was a waste of time to walk

outside the city of Athens because he could not converse with the trees. It's rather a pity that he never tried communicating with nature; I would have loved to read that dialogue.

The longer I walk, the less I differentiate between my body, my mind and my surroundings. The external and internal worlds overlap. I am no longer an observer *looking* at nature, but the entirety of my body is involved.

   Both nature and your body are comprised of the same elements. Oxygen, carbon, nitrogen and hydrogen. It should therefore be natural for the body to become dynamic and interactive in relation to the landscape. When this happens, one experiences what Maurice Merleau-Ponty described as a "lived perspective." Your surroundings and your body find a common language and are transformed into a unity larger than themselves. There are several ways in which one might experience this kind of feeling. You could fast, meditate, take a pill, or pray. But for me, it's walking.

*

Immanuel Kant, who preferred a short walk every day at 3:30 p.m., struck a slightly similar chord—and inspired Merleau-Ponty—in his book with the wonderful title *Dreams of a Spirit-Seer*. If we are going to attempt a description of where the soul is, we should say: "Where I sense, there I am. I am just as immediately in the tips of my fingers, as in my head . . . my soul is as a whole in my whole body, and wholly in each part."

A practical *I walk* prefaces the Cartesian *I think*.

Sometimes when I am out on a long trek, feeling cold and exhausted, I might dream about sitting at home in my living room, reading, perhaps watering my flowers; it's a sweet and fine thought but never one that compels me to turn around.

*

"How much farther is it?" is one of the questions that I have asked most often. This was presumably one of the first sentences I learned to say. My mother and father took me on hikes as soon as I learned how to walk. I would walk a little way behind them and ask this question. When I went up a steep hill, my father would stand at the top cheering me on—*heia!* When I reached the top, he would turn and keep going. My children have carried on the tradition of this question. They walk a short way in silence and then stop and ask. Continue walking and then ask again.

It's a mistake to think too much about the goal and to ask too often about it. I was happy on those hikes with my parents. Happy that my dad whooped *heia!* or that my mum shared an orange with me. Happy until the moment when I started asking how much farther it was.

Just like Zeno's arrow—the arrow that never reaches its destination after leaving the bow because it is motionless within each individual instant—it feels like I will never reach the endpoint once I start thinking about my goal. *I will never reach the mountain.*

*

The first philosopher we know by name within Mahāyāna Buddhism, Nāgārjuna, believed that time or "the three times" (*trikāla*) do not exist, but are instead a hoax. That which has passed is over; that which has not yet passed has not yet begun; and that which we are walking, in this moment, constitutes infinitely small spaces between the passed and the not-yet-passed, and therefore the present also does not exist. Nāgārjuna also uses walking as a metaphor for time: the past is over, and does not exist; the future has not yet begun, and thus also does not exist; and the present is merely the boundary between the two, which itself has no extent and, therefore, does not exist either—everything is only something that we construe so that we may order our own thoughts. I like pondering such thought experiments as I walk because they turn my experience of the world on its head.

"Do you believe that the future can occur several times?" the father asks his son in Paolo Cognetti's novel *The Eight Mountains*. The two are hiking in the

Italian Alps and the father puts a different spin on time than Nāgārjuna does. "That is difficult to say," the son replies. "Do you see the river?" the father continues. "Let us imagine that the water is time passing. If the river is the present here where we are standing, where do you think the future is?" The son answers, as I also did when reading the novel, that the future is downriver from where they are standing. The time that is to come follows the stream of water down the valley. The father replied curtly that this was incorrect. Later that evening, as the boy was about to go to sleep, he began to understand what the father had meant. If the place where you are standing is the present, the past is the water that has flowed past you and beyond, which you will never again see. The future is the water that comes from above, bringing with it dangers, joys and surprises. "Whatever fate awaits," the boy thinks, "it stays up there in the mountains, high up above our heads."

After walking in solitude towards the South Pole for forty days, I made the same mistake that I did when

I was younger. I began to mentally calculate how much time I had left to go. Ten days times ten hours per day of walking would be 100 hours. At first I felt glad, but then this feeling changed. The next day, I wrote in my journal: "The South Pole went from being a distant, good dream to a mathematical point. This or that many hours left." I was depressed at the thought of all the hours that remained. My mood altered my experience of the natural surroundings, and suddenly the wilderness seemed "drab and endlessly monotonous in its whiteness. No energy left to inject life into it." I was disappointed at how whiny I got. It wasn't until late the following day that my negative thoughts no longer held sway and the pleasure of being under way returned.

I hear stories like this all the time. Long-time prisoners who manage to withstand the inhumane jail system often express the same sentiments as polar explorers on their way to the goal: take one day at a time. When I started my publishing house in 1996, I didn't think very far ahead. My colleagues and I had to fight to keep our heads above water, publish good books and sell as many as we could every day. I lacked the time and resources for grander visions. I had learned a thing or two from all of those miles on foot, and was able to simply take one step at a time.

*

A friend of mine who also likes walking is Fernando García-Dory, a Spanish shepherd and artist. The shepherd culture in the world is under threat, and so in recent years he's tried to preserve the vocation by educating and training shepherds. One of the finest treks he knows of is when the sheep are herded through Spain from north to south or vice versa, depending on the season. The trek takes two months to complete. One evening he sat shooting the breeze with a colleague about their joys in life, and the other shepherd told him: "When you go walking with the sheep, and you see they walk, they run, they eat what they like, they keep moving, free, getting healthier, stronger. You see the lambs getting fatter. When you see the flock happy, then, even when you make the camp every night, tired after many miles of walking, you also feel good, happy and more relaxed."

Fernando has accompanied many different nomadic people on journeys throughout the world. For Tuaregs, Berber nomads of the Sahara, happiness is found at the next oasis. For them, there is little difference between their desire and the goal of their profession. Fernando has posed the same question to everyone who crosses his path: "Imagine you close your eyes and open them again in twenty years. What would you be happy to see?"

The answers are similar, whether among the Samburu, or the Maasai from Tanzania and Kenya, or various tribes of Rajasthan. Everyone thinks that what would make them happiest is to see their flocks healthy and fat. They imagine families together, relaxing and enjoying nature, which would be rich and fertile. "That's the harmony," says Fernando, "for those who wish to live in balance with nature. Instead of focusing on their individual needs, they look after the common needs, those of the community, in its expanded sense. From a son to a tree to a sheep." The answers mirror a longing to feel that we are part of something larger than ourselves. Not only society, which is important enough, but something more. Nature has its own intelligence. In school, I learned that the spiritual was the opposite of the material, but in the woods these two are not opposites—they are equals. To walk reflects this.

*

On Saturdays and Sundays, I like to walk for a few hours in the Nordmarka woods. Not to get from one place to another, but simply to walk. I sit down at the bottom of the stairs in my home at Blindern. In the door there is a north-facing window. It allows a glimpse of the woods. On my shoe stand there's a heap of old trainers. I use shoes until they are worn out. Brand, fit and soles are not very important when the surface is moss, roots, soil and heather. I choose a pair, lace them up and walk across the Gaustad field into the woods. Preferably off the beaten track. To walk—to take one step at a time—can be about loving the earth, seeing yourself and letting your body travel at the same speed as your soul.

When I'm out in the woods, I feel how I gradually become part of my surroundings. It feels as if my body doesn't stop at my fingertips. When the hours pass, I become one with the grass, the heather, the trees and the air. If a bird has hurt its wing or an animal has gone hungry, I feel some of their pain. A ray of sunlight finding its way through the foliage and touching my face feels like a tiny miracle. Then I become part of something all-encompassing—so much more than I do as a publisher and family man. It's not a wish to run away from the latter, but to be part of the former. After spending thirty days alone in Antarctica, I wrote in my diary: "I have felt more alone at parties than I do out here." I could yearn for people, skin contact, someone to hold, but the yearning was lessened when the snow and ice, the horizon, the cold and the clouds gradually became part of me. Was this feeling an indication of what people who truly live their everyday lives in tune with nature feel on a daily basis? Perhaps. I love the society I'm part of, and the demands it makes on me. But I think we will be wise to take notice of the experiences Fernando mentioned. They have, after all, been around for thousands of years.

If I walk in the opposite direction, towards the city, it is harder to acknowledge this, but not impossible. The tempo is faster, the expectations and disturbances tenfold. Had I been born in a really large city, I might have understood this better.

*

I remember that in school, they strived for objectiveness. Tasks had a beginning and an end, tests got graded, and behaviour had a norm. To walk is about something else. You can reach your goal, only to continue walking the next day. A hike may last a lifetime. You can walk in one direction and end up at your starting point.

*

Is it possible to wake up on the top of Mount Everest the morning after you've gone to sleep at home in your own bed? After a walk with Arne Næss I have to say that it's not impossible.

The first time I remember something impossible happening was on 20 July 1969. Neil Armstrong walked on the Moon and the USA won the race to be the first nation to make a footprint on our closest planet. A footprint that has not been swept away, seeing as there is never any wind on the Moon. I was six years old and I ran outside to stare and stare at the Moon, certain that I could see Armstrong. After taking a few of his strange, floating steps, Armstrong turned, raised his Hasselblad and photographed Buzz Aldrin climbing out of *The Eagle*. Aldrin was upset for the rest of his life that Armstrong got to walk on the Moon before him. In addition, Armstrong was the one who spoke the sentence that the whole world remembers. Aldrin reminds me that anything, even walking on the Moon, can be remembered as a defeat.

I asked the American astronaut Kathy Sullivan what she thought when she saw our planet far away, while

getting ready to walk in space: "In our everyday lives, we know 'Earth' as the small patch of ground in which we live our lives. When you reach orbit, you suddenly see 'Earth' as what it is: one planet. A single sphere on which we all live." Her respect for our planet suddenly increased.

How did it feel to walk in space? "I was one thousand per cent in the moment . . . with only a faint thought in the back of my mind for how cool it was to be doing this in the real world [rather than another practice session]."

Around the turn of the century, I travelled with Arne Næss to the islands of Micronesia. Far off, in the middle of the ocean, is Nan Madol, a forgotten city in the Western Pacific Ocean that is reminiscent of Venice. The city was constructed on a coral reef with stones below as the foundation and woodwork above. The work began around the 600s and was completed during the 1200s, about the same time that Notre-Dame was being constructed in Paris, and Angkor Wat in Cambodia. Today, the foundations of

several of the ninety-two man-made islands protrude above the surface of the ocean. They consist of 750,000 tons of black basalt boulders weighing between five and ten tons each. The boulders were most likely taken from a quarry located at a distance of about twelve miles away. Researchers wonder how the rocks were transported. Were they dragged through the jungle? After trying to walk across the island ourselves, we doubted that humans could have managed such a feat. Were the boulders carried by canoe? No one can say.

The construction of Nan Madol remains one of the world's greatest archaeological mysteries to this day. According to island legend, a dragon carried all the rocks from the quarry to the site, where the same dragon then stacked them neatly, one on top of the other. One professor of archaeology, who travelled together with us, gave his brief response to the legend: "It is impossible, impossible, impossible." Arne looked at him thoughtfully and then replied: "It is completely possible but, when considered with our conventional calculations, extremely unlikely.

Philosophically, there is a chasm between the impossible and the fantastically unlikely."

I was very grateful for those two sentences because Arne was able to put into words something that I had sensed, but was unable to express. To claim that everything is possible can, logically, be just as correct as claiming that everything is impossible. When I am doing a long hike or climbing a mountain, I might have a great degree of control, but I will never have absolute control. Doubt is good for opportunities. "Claiming that something is impossible is nothing more than a temporary working hypothesis," said Arne. Two plus two can equal five *if* something changes. He said this often, and referred to this way of thinking as *possibilism*, usually with a smile playing on his lips. I don't think that Arne Næss actually believed that he might wake up on the summit of Mount Everest after falling asleep in his own bed in Midtstuen in Oslo, but he would not have considered it an absolute impossibility.

*

"Don't do it" and "This is never going to work out" are two commandments that I heard often while growing up. Sometimes they were right—I wasn't able to walk as far as I had hoped, and it was then that I experienced one of the stupidest of all self-motivating emotions: *Schadenfreude*—but on other occasions, things turned out just fine. If you tell your five-year-old daughter that she's no good at running, she is most likely going to believe that for the rest of her life.

I was never the fastest cross-country skier or the strongest participant in a school competition. I was the worst student in class year after year and received terrible grades in gym. Today, I know that the two most important reasons why I have been able to complete long walking trips on skis are that I prepared well and I tried. I had a bit of luck in that no one else had yet managed to walk alone to the South Pole. Getting there was easier than I thought it would be. It felt like a small miracle, like the time my brother and I found our way out of the Østmarka woods around Oslo after we had got ourselves lost. Arne Næss was right in claiming, "Every now and then, the unimaginable happens to us."

*

Homo sapiens didn't invent bipedalism. It was the
other way around. *Australopithecus*, our forefathers,
had already been walking for over two million years
when our particular species came into being.
Everything that we do today, that which separates
us from other species, can be traced back to our origins
of walking.

The ability to walk, to put one foot in front of the
other, invented *us*.

The driving force ever since the time that
Australopithecus stood upright on two legs until
humankind walked on the Moon and onwards through
history, until the day my daughter Solveig learned to
walk, has remained the same: we are born explorers.

If *Homo sapiens* had not been a walking species, we
would have died out long ago, or lived much like other
animals. We would have crawled around without the
languages we have today.

If we walk less, we are no longer a species
characterized by the fact that we walk, but rather by
the fact that we sit, and that we drive. It's a bit like the

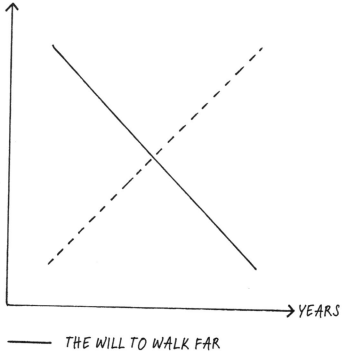

YEARS

———— THE WILL TO WALK FAR

- - - - THE ABILITY TO WALK FAR

Pixar characters in *WALL-E*—which takes place eight hundred years from now—who sit on chairs and drive themselves around, fat and happy on board a spaceship, ignorant at first of their surroundings.

I have started to wonder whether it might have been a mistake to call us *Homo sapiens. Sapiens* means "knowing, able," or in other words, "wise or clever." Self-designated labels that are self-amplifying tend to be a bit exaggerated. The idea is that *Homo sapiens* has developed so much more than every other species on the planet and that we will continue to remain superior to other species. I am not sure.

We should rather be called *Homo insipiens. Insipiens* is a negation of *sapiens* and means "*not* knowing." While *Homo sapiens* seems one-dimensional and sedated, *Homo insipiens* indicates, for me, a broader meaning that I think better reflects who we are: we are seeking knowledge.

One natural question to ask that follows all this is whether we—by ceasing to walk—might eventually develop by degrees into something other than what we currently consider human?

A life spent sitting becomes less physical. We will start to experience the world in another way, namely, we won't experience it—we won't even sense our surroundings—in the way that is only possible when one walks. The tastes, smells, what we see and feel and hear, will be viewed with a different set of contents. Existence will become more abstract. Like the figures in WALL-E, we will literally be out of touch and ungrounded. Instead of physically experiencing our surroundings, getting to know yourself and your environment in the interface between your body and the world, it will become more and more natural to seek out mental experiences and thereby maybe open ourselves to less tangible things, such as religions and emotions.

Could this be true? Fully aware of my own limitations, I wrote to the neurologist Edvard Moser, winner of a Nobel Prize for medicine, and asked whether we could evolve into more abstract beings. I

questioned whether our understanding of being a part
of the whole world could shift to being more about
thoughts than about physical proximity. Moser
answered: "Yes, that makes a lot of sense," and he
emphasized that what happens if we stop walking will
depend on what takes its place. "It is indeed possible
to compensate for most things if one has learned to
walk at a young age, and then stops walking. But
walking and movement also constitute the basis for
exploration, and exploration is the basis for our
intellect."

In Sanskrit, walking is not only a metaphor for *time* but
also for "knowing"—or *gati*. We have this metaphor in
Norwegian, and in a sense it is in English too. In
Norwegian, we say that we have *gjennomgått*
something, which literally means to "walk through,"
but this expression in Norwegian has the same
meaning as the English "to go through" something,
implying knowledge following an experience. The
people who created Sanskrit have managed to clarify

this much better than in Norwegian or English, making up a specific rule: *sarve gatyarthā jñānārthāś ca*—every word that means "walk" also means to "know."

I am not surprised that an ancient Indian language and the Norwegian language agree on the meanings of *to walk* and *to know*. The similarities between the meaning of these words follow the age-old kinships around the world and tell of the experiences that people have gathered as they have travelled. That is beautiful.

Walking made it possible for us to become who we are, so if we hardly ever walk, we may become something else.

*

The last walk that my grandfather—Morfar—took was to face a firing squad at the Akershus Fortress on the morning of 9 February 1945. The German occupying powers had sentenced him to death. "If I had known that it would end like this, I would have done more," he told the judges when they read out his sentence. He had been a lawyer in Oslo, while secretly working for the Resistance, and spoke fluent German. The Nazis could not find any proof of his connections, but it did not matter. He had heard a rumour earlier in the day that he was going to be arrested and subsequently executed, but he knew that if he tried to escape, another Norwegian would be killed in his place, for revenge. Morfar did not entertain any thoughts of getting away and leaving someone else to die in his place. He allowed himself to be arrested. I believe that everyone in our family has asked themselves whether they would have made the same choice on that day, or whether they would have tried to hide. These are the kinds of questions that you don't know the answer to until they are staring you in the face. My grandmother—Mormor—never got over it, she never remarried and her sorrow remained lodged in her body for the next fifty-six years.

He had three daughters at home, just as I do. I have tried to imagine the way in which he took those last few steps. Did the eight Norwegian Nazis who stood waiting to shoot feel happy at the sight of a broken man walking his last few steps to the execution site? A man who they could mock? Or did he manage to walk with a confident forward motion and perhaps show that, though they might murder entire crowds, their struggle would always be in vain?

*

Notes

Walking is based primarily upon things I have seen, felt and heard while on foot, in addition to books and articles I have read upon returning home.

I read about children, movement and related research in the *Guardian:* theguardian.com/environment/2016/mar/25 /three-quarters-of-uk-children-spend-less-time-outdoors -than-prison-inmates-survey. The increasing pollution in Delhi is written about every winter: www.independent.co.uk /news/world/asia/delhi-india-suffers-second-smog-crisis -12-months-as-wakeup-calls-go-unheeded-pollution -a8068831.html.

The English translation of Robert Walser's *The Walk* is by Christopher Middleton with Susan Bernofsky (New Direction Pearls: 2012). The quotes from Milan Kundera are taken from *Slowness*, translated by Linda Asher (Harper Perennial: 1997).

The word *saudade* is used slightly differently in Portugal, Cape Verde and Brazil. The Portuguese writer and soldier

Manuel de Melo defined it as: "a pleasure you suffer, an ailment you enjoy."

The essayist Michel de Montaigne's account of Aesop's question is in *Montaigne & Melancholy: The Wisdom of the Essays* by M. A. Screech (Rowman & Littlefield Publishers: 2000, p. 137). The anecdote about Kaiser Conrad III is found in "We reach the same end by different means" in *Essays, Book I* by Montaigne, translated by Peter Millican: http://www.earlymoderntexts.com/assets/pdfs /montaigne1580book1.pdf.

Montaigne wrote about nearly every topic, and when I write about how pain can be purposeful and joyful, it is something that he has also touched upon (*On Experience*, volume III). The quote on pain by Arthur Schopenhauer is from Schopenhauer's "On the Variety and Suffering of Life," published in *Happiness: Classic and Contemporary Readings in Philosophy*, edited by Steven M. Cahn and Christine Vitrano (Oxford University Press: 2008).

I have drawn from numerous articles on forest bathing—it's already a trend—but these two in particular: https://

www.ncbi.nlm.nih.gov/pubmed/24858508 and https://
qz.com/804022/health-benefits-japanese-forest-bathing/.

The researcher Yoshifumi Miyazaki, to whom I refer,
works as Director of the Center for Environment, Health
and Field Sciences at Chiba University.

Henry David Thoreau is one of the most central proponents
of walking. I took great pleasure in reading his short book
Walking, as well as *The Journal of Henry David Thoreau,
1837–1861* (NYRB Classics: 2009) and *The Essays of Henry David
Thoreau* (Library of America: 2001). The quotes are taken
from these sources.

Kathleen Rooney's novel *Lillian Boxfish Takes a Walk* was
published by St. Martin's Press in 2017.

The Norwegian philosopher Peter Wessel Zapffe wrote about
how we censor our own experiences in his book *On the
Tragic*, which has not yet been translated in its entirety into
English. The English quote referenced here was drawn from
a translation of *The Last Messiah* found online at *Philosophy
Now*, originally published in *Janus #9*, 1933, and translated
from the Norwegian by Gisle R. Tangenes: https://
philosophynow.org/issues/45/The_Last_Messiah.

Melissa Harrison's book *RAIN: Four Walks in English Weather* was published by Faber & Faber in 2016.

The four lines from William Wordsworth's *The Prelude*, 1805, Book Seventh, "Residence in London," are freely available online. Wordsworth was a frequent walker and wrote about his experiences. The poem consists of 645 lines.

Accompanying me on the trek through Los Angeles were Peder Lund and Petter Skavlan. Petter wrote a diary and I have used it to recollect details from the walk.

I spoke with and exchanged emails with the neurological researcher Kaja Nordengen in the summer of 2017 regarding the way in which our walking tempo influences our brain function.

The English quotation from Genesis is taken from the Revised Standard Version (RSV) at https://www.bible gateway.com.

I read about the author Vladimir Nabokov's teachings on Joyce's *Ulysses* in *The New Yorker* magazine. The article was written by Ferris Jabr: http://www.newyorker.com/tech /elements/walking-helps-us-think. I also read about this in an article in *Vogue* (1969) by Allene Talmey: http://www.lib.ru /NABOKOW/Inter14.txt_with-big-pictures.html. The quotes are from these two sources.

In the spring of 1986, I sailed to the Juan Fernández islands from Bermuda, and through the Panama Canal on my way to the Antarctic. I was part of the crew on the sailboat *War Baby* and the late Warren Brown was the captain. I heard the anecdote about Selkirk hunting goats on foot from the Norwegian author Lars Mytting. A few simple Internet searches for eyewitness accounts back up the story.

I learned about the research on humans, cockroaches, and also penguins and elephants, while breakfasting with Professor Rory P. Wilson in LA in the fall of 2016. Wilson is far from being the only person to conduct such research, and was careful to mention this. The scientific article that explains these experiments is: "Wild State Secrets: Ultra-sensitive Measurement of Micro-movement Can Reveal Internal Processes in Animals," written by Ed Grundy, Richard Massy, Joseph Soltis, Brenda Tysse, Mark Holton, Yuzhi Cai, Andy Parrott, Luke A. Downey, Lama Qasem and Tariq Butt, in addition to Wilson. The article was first

published by the Ecological Society of America on
1 December 2014.

The research conducted at Stanford is well documented in
multiple sources, including on the university's website:
http://news.stanford.edu/ 2014/04/24/walking-vs-sitting
-042414/; in a *New York Times* article written by Gretchen
Reynolds: https://well.blogs.nytimes.com/2014/04/30
/want-to-be-more-creative-take-a-walk/?r=0; in an article for
the American Psychological Association: "Give Your Ideas
Some Legs: The Positive Effect of Walking on Creative
Thinking" written by Marily Oppezzo and Daniel L. Schwartz;
and in the aforementioned article authored by Ferris Jabr for
The New Yorker magazine. Any quotes or information have
been extracted from these sources.

The dramatic increase in humans' consumption of calories
is described by Yuval Noah Harari in *Homo Deus* (Harvill
Secker: 2016) and Ian Morris in *Why the West Rules for Now:
The Patterns of History, and What They Reveal About the Future*
(Profile Books: 2011). The latter describes the phenomenon
in detail with excellent tables that are able to show much
more than this essay was able to go into.

Tomas Espedal's *Tramp: Or the Art of Living a Wild and Poetic Life* was translated by James Anderson (Seagull Books: 2010).

I read W. G. Sebald's *Austerlitz* in Norwegian long before I considered writing on the topic of walking. I was reminded of the book when I read James Wood's article "W. G. Sebald, Humorist" in *The New Yorker:* http://www.newyorker.com /magazine/2017/06/05/w-g-sebald-humorist. Wood writes about how Sebald in the novel describes the morning of Prague's occupation by the Germans: "There are people here, but they are in the process of becoming unpeople," and compares the city's inhabitants with trees that have been felled.

The quotations from Marcel Mauss were from Mauss's "Techniques of the Body" in *Economy and Society* (1973, pp. 70–88). I have taken a great deal of pleasure in discussing both his work and that of Pierre Bourdieu with the Norwegian philosopher Lars Fr. H. Svendsen.

The manner in which the criminal Ted Bundy would evaluate possible victims has been described in numerous sources, but the quotation was taken from: http://www.bbc .com/future/story/20160519-what-your-walk-really-says -about-you.

The conversation with Robert Wilson took place in the early summer of 2017 at my home in Oslo. Our dialogue continued for the ensuing weeks via emails sent between Wilson, his colleague Owen Laub and myself. The woman who taught Wilson to speak was the ballet dancer Byrd Hoffman.

My sources for Maurice Merleau-Ponty's philosophy is *The Phenomenology of Perception* (published originally in France in 1942. I read the edition published by Routledge in 1995, translated into English by Colin Smith) and the article: http://mythosandlogos.com/auPonty.html, as well as other articles. I also discussed his theories with the aforementioned Svendsen and the psychiatrist Finn Skårderud.

After enjoying reading the poems of Olav H. Hauge and Antonio Machado, I was further inspired to read about the two poets by an article in *Dag og tid* (14 March 2008) written by the Spanish teacher Elisabet Vallevik Engelstad. The quotation from Hauge's journal was taken from this. For the sake of clarity: Machado wrote his poem before Hauge.

Hippocrates' interest in walking has been mentioned in countless articles. I am not so surprised by his conclusion, but I am fascinated that he was already warning, 2,400 years ago, about doctors' medical errors. "It is solved by walking" is the direct translation of Diogenes' Latin expression *Solvitur ambulando*. The expression may also be understood to mean that practical methods are preferable to theories. Diogenes went walking often, sometimes with a lighted oil lamp in the middle of the day. He claimed to be searching for "an honest person" in Athens, an undertaking at which he apparently did not succeed.

The quotes by Kierkegaard were taken from his undated letter to Henriette Lund, written in 1847. This and a handful of other letters are reproduced here: http://sks.dk/forside /bd.asp. The one exception is the quote: ". . . robbers and the elite agree on just one thing—living in hiding." I read this in *Wanderlust: A History of Walking* by Rebecca Solnit (Penguin Books: 2001). She read this quote in Kierkegaard's *Journals and Papers* (Indiana University Press: 1978), translated by Howard V. Hong and Edna H. Hong.

I have also found Joakim Garff's book *SAK: Søren Aabye* (*Kierkegaard: A Biography*), published in English by Princeton University Press (2007) and translated by Bruce H. Kirmmse, very helpful in understanding his relationship with walking. Towards the end of the biography, Kierkegaard has been taken ill and is bedridden. He was forced to sell off his apartment and his beloved book collection in order to cover expenses. Some have claimed that Kierkegaard's failing finances caused him to lose his desire for walking, to forget his own advice about walking away from his problems, and to subsequently become sick, confining himself to his bed to die. This story would have suited the purposes of my own essay. However, when I asked Garff in the late summer of 2017 about whether this chain of events might in fact be the case, he refuted the idea: "Whether or not there is a causal link between his critical economic situation and his illness, I dare not draw conclusions; but there can be no doubt that Kierkegaard's lean bank account depressed him. And it is a fact that a depressed will to live increases one's risk of [serious] illness."

I read about the *Dallas Bed Rest and Training Study* and relevant studies at: https://www.ncbi.nlm.nih.gov/pmc /articles/PMC2655009/.

Andrew Bastawrous is my source for the story about Maria, his colleagues and himself. I spoke with Andrew about his work in

LA in the autumn of 2016 and he has since recounted the story via email. Andrew wished to keep the name of his patient anonymous, thus Maria is not the main character's true name.

Andrew Bastawrous is a hero. If you would like to learn more about his work, you can read about it at www.peekvision.org. His work is dependent on financial donations. In the UK: https://www.justgiving.com/peek-vision. In the United States: https://tinyurl.com/peekvision.

I was not able to find out the precise work in which George Mallory originally wrote about the point of climbing; however, the quotation has been reproduced in a number of books and online, always credited to him. I was quite happy when I initially read it, especially because he was the first adventurer I had encountered who did not try to position his expeditions in a larger context in order to excuse and explain his spirit of adventure. Nowadays, hardly anyone sets off on an adventure who does not first and foremost emphasize their research, the environment, charity, children or peace as the driving motivation behind their undertakings. The words written by Mallory's wife are taken from the book *The Wildest Dream* by Mark Mackenzie (John Murray: 2009).

The quotation by Immanuel Kant was found in *Dreams of a Spirit-Seer*, originally *Träume eines Geistersehers, erläutert durch Träume der Metaphysik*, Prussian Academy of Sciences (Kant's collected works, volume II, de Gruyter, Berlin: 1902). The work has to date not been translated into Norwegian. The quotation was thus translated for me by Lars Fr. H. Svendsen. (Immanuel Kant: *Dreams of a Spirit-Seer*: https://archive.org/stream/dreamsofspiritse00kant /dreamsofspiritse00kant_djvu.txt.)

The source for Nāgārjuna and Sanskrit is Professor Jens Braarvig.

I read Paolo Cognetti's *The Eight Mountains* in Norwegian (Kagge Forlag: 2017), translated by Tommy Watz. The bestselling Italian novel is available in English (Harvill Secker: 2018), translated by Simon Carnell and Erica Segre. Although similar stories exist in Buddhist literature, I think that Cognetti's telling here is particularly well done.

The astronaut Kathy Sullivan is quite modest, but she told me about some of her experiences in space when I met her in Singapore in 2007. I exchanged emails with her in connection with this book during the summer of 2017. Sullivan was the first American woman to walk in space.

The neuroscientist Edvard Moser and I emailed each other in the late summer of 2017, and the quotes are taken from this exchange.

I read my *morfar*'s quote in a small book that was published by a friend in his honour (1948).

A few parts of this book, like the story of Store Skagastølstind, the conversation with Fernando García-Dory and my expedition below New York, are based on my books *Philosophy for Polar Explorers* (Pushkin Press: 2006), translated by Kenneth Steven; and *Under Manhattan* (World Editions: 2015), translated by Becky L. Crook.

Acknowledgements

I would like to express my deepest thanks to Joakim
Botten, Gabi Gleichmann, Petter Skavlan, Mary
Mount, Kristin B. Johansen, Lars Fr. H. Svendsen,
Dan Frank, Sonny Mehta, Morten Faldaas, Jan Kjærstad,
Finn Skårderud, Lars Mytting, Knut Olav Åmås, M.M.,
Kaja Nordengen, Bjørn Fredrik Drangsholt, Aslak
Nore, Andrew Bastawrous, Ellen Emmerentze Jervell,
Åsne Seierstad, Rory Wilson, Robert Wilson, Owen
Laub, Aase Gjerdrum, Anne Gaathaug, Edvard Moser,
Solveig Øye, Hanneline Røgeberg, Kathy Sullivan,
Jorunn Sandsmark, Jens Braarvig, Susanne Gretter,
Annabel Merullo, Tim Hutton, David Rothenberg,
Kjetil Østli, Odd Harald Hauge, Marie Aubert, Hans
Petter Bakkcteig, Fernando García-Dory, Bob Shaye,
Shân Morley Jones, Becky L. Crook and everyone at
J. M. Stenersens Forlag and Kagge Forlag.

Images